American Red Cross

PET FIRST AID

CATS AND DOGS

Bobbie Mammato, DVM, MPH

StayWell®

A MedMedia USA Company

StayWell
780 Township Line Road
Yardley, PA 19067

International Standard Book Number 1-58480-293-7

06 07 08 09 / 10 9 8 7 6 5 4 3

DEDICATION

This book is dedicated to Al, Alex, Almond, Annie, Baby Jason, Barney, Bear, Bentley, Berkeley, Blanche, Bomber, Buud, Caitlin Nicole, Carmel, Cassie, Chip, Chipper, Cinder, Clementine, Cleo, Coal, Coco, Durham, Ebony, Esau, Fax, Figgan, Felix, Fleetwood, Gator, Gertie, Giorgio, Gizmo, Grizabella, Gus, Hank, Jack, Jacob, Jake, Jasmine, Jeremiah, Joey, Josephine, Juanita, Kashiri, Kelsey, Leader, Lewis, Lil Kitty, Lilly, Lou, Lucky, Luke, Madison, Makia, Mickey, Midnight, Mischa, Mr. Bud, Mitz, Molé, Molly, Nuit, Oreo, Oscar, Otto, Piezo, Richard, Ricky, Rosey, Sadie, Sandy, Scrappy, Sebastian, Shadow, Smidge, Sniper, Sunshine, The Dawg, Thorndike, Topaz, Trilby, Ziggy, Zorg, and all the other cats and dogs who depend upon us to help them in times of emergency.

[handwritten notes:]

6-7am + weekends
Emergency Animal Clinic
272-9611
St. Rd. 23

Poison control
800-222-1222

Not 911

ACKNOWLEDGEMENTS

This book was developed and produced through the combined effort of the American Red Cross, external reviewers, and StayWell. Without the commitment to excellence of both employees and volunteers, this book could not have been created.

American Red Cross national headquarters Health and Safety Services staff included Violet Bierce, Earl Harbert, Dana Jessen, Ferris D. Kaplan, Susan M. Livingstone, Rocky Lopes, Heather McMurtrie, Jane E. Moore, Andrea Morisi, Sharon Ritter Smith, Paul Stearns, Jean Wagaman, and S. Elizabeth White.

REVIEWERS

Review was provided by the following individuals:

Jan Bober
Director, Health and Safety
American Red Cross of Massachusetts Bay
Boston, Massachusetts

Beth Bush
Director, Health and Safety Services
American Red Cross, Williamson County Chapter
Franklin, Tennessee

Bernadine D. Cruz, DVM
Laguna Hills Animal Hospital
Laguna Hills, California

Doc Dixon
Service Center Manager
American Red Cross, Louisville Chapter
Louisville, Kentucky

Charles R. James
Health and Safety Education Specialist,
American Red Cross
Los Angeles, California

Susan E. Leonard, DVM
Clinician, Emergency and Critical Care
Veterinary Institute of Trauma Emergency and Critical Care
at the Animal Emergency Center
Milwaukee, Wisconsin

Elke Rudloff, DVM, DACVECC
Clinical Instructor, Emergency and Critical Care
Veterinary Institute of Trauma Emergency and Critical Care
at the Animal Emergency Center
Milwaukee, Wisconsin

A NOTE TO THE READER

If someone is bitten by a wild or domestic animal, try to get the victim away from the animal without endangering yourself. Do not try to restrain or capture the animal. If the wound is minor, wash it with soap and water, control any bleeding, apply a dressing and take the victim to a doctor or medical facility. If the wound is bleeding heavily, control the bleeding but do not clean the wound. Seek medical attention immediately. The wound will be properly cleaned at a medical facility.

If possible, try to remember what the animal looks like and the area in which the animal was last seen. Call 9-1-1 or the local emergency number. The dispatcher will get the proper authorities, such as the local animal care and control agency, to the scene.

DISCLAIMER

The advice provided in this book has been reviewed carefully for safety concerns, but working with or caring for animals, especially sick, wounded or otherwise stressed animals, is inherently unpredictable. Nether the author nor the American Red Cross takes responsibility for failures of or complications arising from any of the procedures described in this book, or for any injury or illness to any person or animal, or for damage to property resulting from any of the advice or direction contained in the book. Guidelines are based on experience and current medical information, however their use may not provide the results intended and no claim is made that their use is without risk. This book is not intended to be a substitute for care by a veterinarian, and pet owners are encouraged to seek emergency veterinary care as soon as possible after an injury or emergency.

It should also be noted that even application of the most advanced technology and veterinary expertise is not always successful, and emergency care given at home or on the scene of an accident is likely to have an even lower rate of success.

ABOUT THE ILLUSTRATIONS

Pet First Aid includes quite a few illustrations to help you understand how to best care for your pet. These illustrations refer to selected information and directions, as well as to specific steps for a given procedure. You should note that not all steps are illustrated—just those that prove the biggest help to you in applying the information included here.

ABOUT THE AUTHOR

Dr. Bobbie Mammato earned her veterinary degree from the New York State College of Veterinary Medicine at Cornell University, and completed an internship in Emergency and Critical Care Medicine at the Veterinary Institute of Trauma, Emergency and Critical Care Medicine in Milwaukee, Wisconsin. She received a Masters in Public Health degree from The Johns Hopkins University School of Hygiene and Public Health.

In addition to her concentration in emergency and critical care medicine and epidemiology, Dr. Mammato's experience includes work in the clinics of several humane organizations and teaching at the college level. She currently serves as disaster relief consultant to The Humane Society of the United States and practices small animal medicine on a part-time basis. She lives with her husband Barry, son Noah, four cats and a dog.

CONTENTS

INTRODUCTION

A VETERINARIAN'S PERSPECTIVE

As a veterinarian, I know the undeniable strength of the human-animal bond. For many of us it is so strong that our pets are considered a part of our family. My training in Emergency and Critical Care Medicine and Public Health has taught me the importance of alerting the public to the many warning signs and common household hazards that signal danger, and the importance of preparing for a pet's illness or injury. Every year in the United States millions of people become certified in cardiopulmonary resuscitation (CPR), and as a result countless human lives have been saved. Now is the time to consider what happens when an emergency threatens our other loved ones—our pets.

Bobbie Mammato, DVM, MPH

FROM THE AMERICAN RED CROSS

At the American Red Cross our mission is to help people prevent, prepare for, and respond to emergencies and disasters. Governed by volunteers and supported by community donations, the American Red Cross is a nationwide network of nearly 900 locally supported chapters, annually mobilizing relief to families affected by more than 70,000 disasters. We are also the largest supplier of blood and blood products to more than 3,000 hospitals across the nation.

Training almost 12 million people in lifesaving skills each year, we help people learn how to save lives and prepare for emergencies of all types. The Red Cross is the leader in providing lifesaving skills such as first aid, cardiopulmonary resuscitation (CPR), and teaching laypersons and professionals how to use automated external defibrillators (AEDs) to save victims of sudden cardiac arrest. In addition, the Red Cross leads the way by developing aquatic safety, learn-to-swim, and lifeguard-training programs used in communities across the country. The Red Cross constantly strives to respond to the health and safety concerns of Americans at home, in school, and in the workplace by providing products, training, and information for situations faced in today's environment.

American Red Cross National Headquarters
2025 E Street, N.W.
Washington, D.C. 20006
www.redcross.org

1

EMERGENCY PROTOCOLS

HOW TO APPROACH A SICK OR INJURED DOG OR CAT

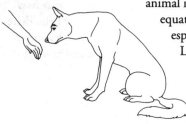

Always approach a sick or injured animal slowly and cautiously. Even your own sweet pet, who would never otherwise be aggressive, may strike out when frightened or in pain. Dog and cat bites are serious injuries; getting bitten does not help the animal in need, it only adds one more problem to the equation. Keep an eye on posture and expressions— especially the animal's face, ears, tail, fur and body. Listen to the sounds being made. As you approach, allow the animal to smell the back of your hand. Watch for reactions carefully; never make quick, jerky or loud movements. Allow the animal to see what you are doing.

TIP: *Always speak in a soft, soothing tone to an injured or sick animal. Avoid direct eye contact—some animals may perceive it as a threat.*

Body Language Warning Signs

Growling; hair on shoulders, back and hind end standing up; snarling with teeth exposed and upper lips lifted up; ears forward; tail may be wagging slightly.

or...

Ears straight back against the head, tail tucked between legs and may snarl and have the hair on the back raised.

or...

Crouched with tail between legs and ears flat, dog assumes a submissive posture, such as lying on the side with belly exposed; may also make licking movements or urinate. These are signs of submission, but a fearfully submissive dog can quickly become a biting dog if you continue to approach.

Cat crouches with ears flattened to the head; the animal may salivate or spit. Pupils may be small, but may become enlarged as the cat becomes more frightened. Back may be arched with tail up, hair is standing up and cat is hissing.

Alternatively, the cat appears to walk on the toes with the head and tail held down, hair partially standing up, ears standing up and pointed so they open on the sides. Whiskers are turned forward and claws are out.

Any of these behaviors may result in the dog or cat attempting to bite. Do not attempt treatment on an animal exhibiting these warning signs!

Even with years of experience and the assistance of trained handlers, veterinarians must sometimes sedate an animal before examination. You don't help an animal by getting hurt yourself. *If you cannot safely handle an animal, call your local animal shelter or animal care and control agency.* While waiting for the arrival of help, there are things you can safely do to help the animal, such as diverting traffic if an animal has been hit by a car and is still in the street, or keeping other people and animals away.

Capture Techniques

Always allow animals to know where you are so you don't surprise them.

- *Leashes.* Leather, nylon or canvas leashes are strong and easy to use for restraining an animal. (Do not use chain-link leashes.)

  1. Make a large loop in a leash by passing the end you normally connect to a collar through the hole in the handle.

  Step 1

  2. Standing just behind or to the side of the animal's head, drop the large loop over the neck and tighten.

  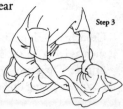

  Step 2

  - *Towels or blankets.* Gently dropping a towel over a cat's body will often subdue the cat.

  1. Drop the towel while standing well above and behind the cat.

  2. Make sure you know the position of the cat as you place the towel so you don't put your hands near the cat's mouth.

  Step 3

  3. Grasp the scruff of the neck so the cat cannot turn around and bite your hand through the towel.

  Step 1

4. Wrap the towel completely around the cat's body and legs, covering all four paws, leaving only the head out of the towel. This allows you to work with the head without four scratching legs going in all directions.

Step 4

- **Boxes.** Cats will often crawl into boxes for comfort; you can use a box to transport the cat or to help you administer treatment.

    1. If the cat goes into a plastic carrier that can come apart, simply remove the top of the carrier.

    2. Drop a towel over the cat.

    3. Perform treatments.

    The box technique may also be used with small dogs that are under 30 pounds.

- **Gloves.** Many people use thick gloves to handle cats and dogs, but you lose dexterity and most glove material can eventually be bitten through. It is important, however, to wear latex gloves whenever possible in order to decrease your exposure to blood and other bodily fluids.

 In the sections that follow, even if it is not explicitly stated, you should wear latex gloves when performing all procedures.

Muzzles

Because all animals who are injured, in pain, sick or scared have the potential to bite, they should be muzzled before any care is attempted. There are some situations in which muzzling may be dangerous to the animal; this danger must be weighed against the risk of human injury. It may be dangerous to muzzle an animal who is:

- Vomiting
- Coughing
- Having difficulty breathing

 Some animals will resist being muzzled and might become aggressive. In this case, do not attempt treatment yourself. Take the animal to your veterinarian or seek help from your local animal shelter or animal care and control agency.

Muzzles can be purchased at pet stores, veterinary hospitals and through pet catalogs. They come in various sizes and should be part of your first aid kit. (See *First Aid Kit*, page 89.) Muzzles may be made of the following:

- Soft nylon material that snaps behind the ears. These are collapsible and easily washed.

- Leather which is stiff and has straps which hook into pre-made holes.

• A combination of leather or plastic sides with straps that hook behind the head and a metal or plastic mesh center. (This is called a *cage muzzle*.) The advantage of this type of muzzle is that the animal can easily breathe through it and vomit if necessary.

There are also pre-made muzzles specifically designed for short-nosed dogs and cats.

Home-made Muzzles

If necessary, you can make a home-made muzzle on the spot. For dogs, except those with very short noses (such as pugs or boxers), follow these steps:

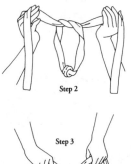

Step 2

1. Start with a piece of material at least 18 inches long. Gauze works best, but a stocking, necktie, sock, soft rope or piece of cloth can be used.

2. Place a knot in the middle of the material. This acts as an anchor for the muzzle.

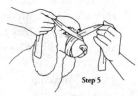

Step 4

Step 3

3. Make a loop large enough to drop over the animal's nose; keep enough distance between you and the animal's mouth so the dog or cat cannot turn around and bite you. Slip the loop over the nose from above and behind the animal's head. Always allow the animal to know where you are at all times.

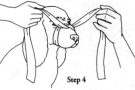

Step 5

4. Tighten the loop down on top of the nose, but not so tight that you interfere with the animal's breathing.

5. Pull an end of the material down each side of the face, criss-cross it under the chin and bring the ends back behind the ears.

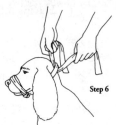

Step 6

6. Tie the loose ends in a bow behind the ears.

For short-nosed dogs and cats, after steps 1–5, take one end of the material and pass it under the loop over the nose and tie it to the other end around the neck.

No muzzle is fool-proof; don't be lulled into a false sense of security while using one. Many dogs and cats can get out of them, especially if not fitted correctly or not tied snugly.

Restraint Techniques

Dog

The first two techniques for restraining dogs require two people—one to hold, while the other performs the treatments. None of these techniques should be attempted without the animal first being muzzled.

- *Headlock*

    1. Place a forearm under the dog's neck and bring the arm up the other side of the neck and around the animal's head.

    2. Face your head toward the animal's back.

    3. Firmly lock your forearm under your head.

    4. Place your other arm over or under the animal's belly.

Large, powerful dogs can't turn around to bite, but can still get up and overpower you. Be particularly careful with small dogs with pushed-in noses, such as pugs; if you hold the neck too tight, you can actually cause the eyes to pop out of their sockets.

- *Lying on their side*

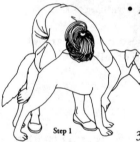

Step 1

Step 3

    1. Stand with your body along the dog's side, facing the dog.

    2. Reach over the top and then under the dog to take hold of the front and hind legs closest to your body.

    3. Gently pull the legs towards you. As the animal drops to the floor, take care not to let the head hit the floor.

    4. Use your legs as a cushion for the fall if you are working on the floor.

    5. Hold the front and hind legs that touch the floor straight out (this prevents the animal from getting up), while using your forearm closest to the animal's head to firmly push the neck down against the surface on which you are working. The legs held straight and the neck pushed down are what keep the animal lying down.

Step 5

- *If you are working alone*

    1. Place a muzzle.

    2. Put the dog on a leash and use it to restrain the dog's head.

    3. Work on the affected area.

Cat

- *Lying on their side.* The technique described above for laying a dog down can also be used on a cat, with a variation: Follow steps 1–4 of *Lying on their side,* on the previous page. At step 5, instead of pushing the head and neck towards the surface the cat is lying on, grasp the skin behind the cat's neck (the scruff) and hold it firmly.

Scruff and sit. An alternate technique.

1. Grasp and hold firmly a large amount of the loose skin (the scruff) behind the cat's neck.

2. With your other hand, hold the cat's body in a sitting position.

TIP: *Use caution whenever you're trying to restrain or capture an animal—even your own. Any injured or frightened animal may try to bite or scratch.*

- *Minimal restraint.* Some cats are more easily managed with minimal restraint and gentle handling, and actually become more difficult to handle with the above techniques. This will have to be assessed on an individual basis.

Choose the appropriate restraint technique, level of restraint and parts of body restrained after assessing the extent and location of injury!

Carrying and Transporting Techniques

If you suspect a back injury, see Back, Broken, *page 26 for the proper transport technique. You may also need to refer to* Restraint Techniques, *page 5.*

Dog

- Small (30 pounds or less)
  - *Arms.* Carry the dog in your arms.
    1. Cradle the dog in your arm.
    2. Place your hand around the dog's front legs, with two or three fingers between the legs.
    3. Hold the legs as you walk.
    4. The injured side should be against your body.
  - *Box.* Carry the dog in a box or carrier.

- Medium or Large

  1. Place one arm under and around the neck.

  2. Cup the other arm behind the hind legs (if you suspect abdominal injury).

  3. Cup the other arm under the belly (if you suspect hind-leg injury).

Cat

- *Arms.* Use the small-dog technique.
- *Scruff.* An alternate technique.

  1. Grasp the loose skin behind the cat's neck with one hand.

  2. Support the cat's body with your other hand.

- *Box.* Cats should be transported in a box or carrier of some kind because they frighten easily and may jump out of your arms.

ADMINISTERING MEDICATION

Liquids

For many people, giving liquid medication to a pet is easier than giving pills. Keep a baby dosing syringe or eye dropper (both with measurements marked) in your first aid kit (see *First Aid Kit,* page 89). You can find these in pharmacies or in the baby section of grocery stores.

- 1 milliliter (ml) = 1 cc
- 5 cc = 1 teaspoon
- 15 cc = 1 tablespoon
- 8 ounces = 1 cup

Technique

1. Place the end of the eye dropper just inside the animal's mouth, where the teeth are shortest and flattest (just behind the canine teeth).

2. Gently position the dropper above the lower teeth, or in the pouch between the gums and lower teeth. (Placing the medicine over the teeth will result in less spitting of the medicine than placing it in the pouch.)

3. Slowly administer the medication, giving it no faster than the animal can swallow.

TIP: *Never administer any medications unless they are prescribed by a veterinarian.*

Pills and Capsules

Technique

1. Hold your pet's upper jaw toward the ceiling by taking hold of the snout and gently pointing it upward. This will cause the lower jaw to drop slightly.

Step 1

2. Gently pull down on the very front-most part of the lower jaw.

3. Place the tablet as far back into the mouth as you safely can, in the center of the back of the tongue.

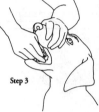
Step 3

4. Hold the mouth closed once you have the pill in it, until your pet swallows or licks their nose. Sometimes, gently blowing on the nose or rubbing the throat will cause the animal to swallow.

Step 4

Pills can also be hidden in food, but you must ensure your pet does not eat the morsel and spit out the pill. For dogs, peanut butter works well because it is sticky and tends to hold the tablet. (Cats generally won't eat peanut butter.) If the animal is vomiting or has diarrhea, hiding medication in food is not a good idea since it may stimulate vomiting.

Wrapping a cat up in a towel so only the head shows may help you avoid getting scratched. See *Capture Techniques*, page 2.

Giving medication with the dog in a sitting position, backed into a corner so the dog can't get up, generally works best.

There are also commercial pill "guns" available. These are plastic tubes that hold the pill and allow you to place it in the back of the throat without putting your hands in the animal's mouth.

Never attempt to give medications by mouth to an animal who is lying down, unconscious, vomiting, aggressive or seizuring.

Administering Eye Medications

Technique

1. Rest the side of the hand which you will use to administer the medication on the bone above the upper eyelid. This will help prevent poking the medication tube into the eye if you are jostled.

2. Tilt the head backward slightly with the palm of your hand under the chin supporting the head.

3. With this same hand, pull down the lower eyelid with your thumb.

4. Place drops or ointment directly on the eye. Be careful not to touch the tip of the dispenser to the eye.

Administering Ear Medication

Technique

1. Stand on the side of the animal, on the same side as the ear you will be treating.

2. If necessary, lift the floppy portion of the ear so you can clearly see inside the ear opening.

3. Place the drops or ointment in the middle of the ear opening.

4. Rub the base of the ear to allow the medication to drop down into the deeper portions of the ear.

RECOGNIZING AN EMERGENCY

The best way to be prepared to recognize and respond to an emergency is to know how your pet usually looks and acts, and to be aware of what situations constitute an emergency.

Emergency Situations

The following situations should be considered emergencies:

- Trauma. Examples include an animal hit by a car, a gunshot wound or an animal fallen from a building or other significant height.
- Difficult breathing.
- Seizures, particularly first seizures, seizures lasting more than two minutes and seizures recurring repeatedly (one after the other).
- Cuts and gashes that cause internal organs to become exposed or fall out.
- Excessive bleeding such as spurting blood, bleeding that is prolonged or that you cannot stop by applying direct pressure.
- Snake bites.
- Heat stroke (hyperthermia) or hypothermia.
- Poisoning.
- Shock.
- Open wounds with visible bone or severe tissue damage.
- Burns.

- Problems giving birth.
- Profuse diarrhea or vomiting.
- Straining to urinate or defecate.
- Unconsciousness.
- Painful, enlarged abdomen.
- Severe depression (characterized by hiding, unresponsiveness or refusing to eat).

In the following sections, you will learn how to deal with these situations on an emergency basis. You should always phone or visit your veterinarian or a veterinary emergency hospital immediately.

Assessing the Emergency Scene

When approaching an emergency, look around for potential hazards that may still exist. For example, if an animal has been hit by a car, before running into the street to help, make sure no other cars are approaching. If your pet is engaged in a fight, don't place any part of your body between the two animals or you are apt to become the next victim.

TIP: *Always have the telephone number of your veterinarian, 24-hour veterinary emergency hospital, National Animal Poison Control Center (page 71) and animal shelter or animal care and control agency readily available!*

LEARN WHAT IS NORMAL FOR YOUR PET

You cannot recognize what is abnormal if you don't know what is normal to begin with. Read the normal values listed below and get to know what normal looks like in your pet. Observe such things as how your pet breathes, eats, drinks, walks, urinates and defecates. Knowing these things about your pet will make you sensitive to changes that may signal problems.

Heart Rate and Pulses

- The heartbeat of a dog or cat can be felt at about the point where the left elbow touches the chest (about the fifth rib).

  1. Lay your pet down on the right side.

  Step 3

  2. Gently bend the left-front leg at the elbow.

  3. Bring the elbow back to where it touches the chest.

4. Place your hand or a stethoscope (available at most pharmacies) over this area to feel or hear and count heartbeats.

- Pulses can also be felt with a light touch using your middle and index finger at three additional locations:

  - *The inner thigh.* This is the easiest of the three locations at which to feel the pulse.

    1. Lay your pet down, on either side.

    2. Gently lift the upper back leg away from the lower back leg.

    3. Place your two fingers as high up as possible on the inside of either leg, just where the leg meets the body wall. A light touch should be used; if you press too hard you will not feel the pulse.

    4. Feel for a pulse. The pulse can be felt in the middle of the leg approximately half way between the front and back of the leg, where you can feel a recess in the leg; this recess is where the blood vessels run.

  - *Just below the wrist* (carpus).

    1. The animal may either sit or lie down.

    2. Locate the area just above the middle pad on the underside of either front paw.

    3. Lightly place your middle and index finger at this point.

    4. Feel for a pulse.

  - *Just below the ankle* (hock).

    1. The animal may either sit or lie down.

    2. Locate the area just above the middle pad on the underside of either hind paw.

    3. Lightly place your middle and index finger at this point.

    4. Feel for a pulse.

Practice on your pet before an emergency occurs!

Normal Heart and Pulse Rates

Dog

- Small, miniature, or toy breed (30 pounds or less): 100–160 beats per minute.
- Medium to large breed (over 30 pounds): 60–100 beats per minute.
- Puppy (until one year old): 120–160 beats per minute.

Cat

- 160–220 beats per minute.

Heart rates outside these ranges could signal an emergency.

Breathing Rate

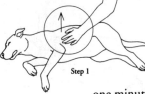 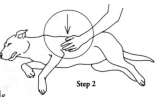

1. Have your pet either stand or lie down.
2. Watch your pet and count the number of times, in one minute, that the chest rises and falls.

Step 1

Step 2

In an emergency situation, if you are not sure whether your pet is breathing, try one of these techniques:

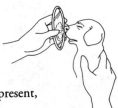

- Hold a cotton ball or tissue just in front of the nostrils and watch it to see if it moves. If it does, your pet is breathing.

- Hold a mirror up to your pet's nose and look for water droplets (condensation). If they are present, your pet is breathing.

Normal Breathing Rates

Dog

- 10–30 breaths per minute.
- Up to 200 pants per minute.

Cat

- 20–30 breaths per minute.
- Up to 300 pants per minute.

Cats do not normally pant unless they are frightened or in distress. Cats should not pant for more than a few minutes at a time. If panting appears to go on longer, treat as an emergency.

Respiratory Pattern

When a dog or cat inhales normally, the chest should expand. If the animal's abdomen is actively expanding instead of the chest, this may indicate a problem. Exhaling should be an easy process; there should be no work involved. *If your pet is making loud, shallow or gasping sounds when breathing, or if your pet is not breathing, it is an emergency. See CPR, page 15.*

Taking Your Pet's Body Temperature

1. See section on *Restraint Techniques,* page 5.
2. Use a pediatric rectal or digital thermometer.
3. If using a mercury thermometer, shake the thermometer to reset it from the last use.
4. Lubricate the thermometer with a water-based lubricant or petroleum jelly.
5. With the animal either standing or lying down, insert the thermometer into the rectum (which is located just beneath the tail) to where the start of the mercury (silver line) is visible on a mercury thermometer or to a point just past the tip on a digital thermometer.

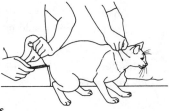

6. Leave the thermometer inserted for three minutes (for a mercury thermometer) or until it beeps (for a digital thermometer).
7. Remove and read where the silver line stops on a mercury thermometer, or simply read the number if using a digital thermometer.

Normal Temperatures

- Dog: 100.2°–102.8° Fahrenheit
- Cat: 100.5°–102.5° Fahrenheit

Temperatures under 100° and over 104° Fahrenheit should be considered an emergency.

Mucous Membrane Color

By observing the color of your pet's mucous membranes, you can determine if enough oxygen is making it into the animal's blood stream. To check the color of the mucous membranes, follow these steps:

1. The animal may be sitting, standing or lying down.
2. Lift the animal's upper or lower lip and observe the color of the gums or inner lip.

Some breeds have black (pigmented) mucous membranes. If this is the case with the animal you are working with, place your thumb on the skin just under the lower eyelid and gently pull down and observe the color of the membranes of the inner lower eyelid.

Normal color is pink—this means the animal's tissues are receiving enough oxygen. *Blue, pale, yellow, white, brick red or brown mucous membrane colors are an emergency.* For additional colors, see first aid for poisoning, page 71.

Capillary Refill Time

This is the time it takes the gums or inner lips to return to their normal pink color after you press them.

1. Your pet may be sitting, standing or lying down.
2. After checking the mucous membrane color, press lightly on the gums or inner lip.
3. Observe the color as it turns white and then pink again. The pink color should return after one or two seconds.

This is a quick way to see if blood circulation is normal. Normal refill time is one to two seconds. *Capillary refill times of less than one second or more than three seconds are an emergency.*

HOW TO DETECT DEHYDRATION

Pull up on the skin at the back of the animal's neck; it should spring back to the normal position immediately (within one or two seconds). If this is delayed, the animal is dehydrated.

Very old (geriatric) and very skinny animals are difficult to assess in this manner because skin loses some of its natural elasticity with age and malnourishment. It is also more difficult to assess dehydration in obese animals. In these circumstances, feel the gums; if they feel dry and sticky, the animal is probably dehydrated. (Note: If the animal is drooling, gums may feel moist despite dehydration.)

Dehydrated animals must be taken to a veterinary hospital for treatment immediately. If you aren't sure whether your pet is dehydrated, the safest option is to take your pet to the veterinarian for an examination.

SURVEY THE EMERGENCY VICTIM

Make an initial evaluation of the medical situation. This initial evaluation ideally should be done in one minute. It consists of doing the following:

- *Inspect the area.* Quickly observe the animal's body; posture; presence of blood, feces, or vomit; breathing pattern; sounds and other materials (possible poisons around the victim).

- *Inspect the animal.* Assess the following:

  - **Airway.** Is there an open airway? If no, see *A= Airway,* page 15.

  - **Breathing.** Is the animal breathing? If no, See *B= Breathing,* page 16.

  - **Circulation.** Is there a heartbeat and a pulse? If no, see *C = Circulation,* page 16.

  - **Mucous membrane color.** See *Mucous Membrane Color,* page 13.

  - **Capillary refill time.** See *Capillary Refill Time,* page 14.

  - **Bleeding.** If the animal is bleeding, see *Bleeding,* page 21.

  - **Level of consciousness.** Is the animal alert, awake, seizuring, disoriented, hyperactive, depressed or unconscious? If the animal is seizuring, See *Seizures,* page 75.

CARDIOPULMONARY RESUSCITATION (CPR AND RESCUE BREATHING)

CPR is the method used to treat an animal who is not breathing or has no heartbeat. It consists of rescue breathing (also called mouth to nose/mouth resuscitation) and chest compressions. CPR is based on three basic principles, called the ABCs of CPR. **You must follow the ABC order (Airway, Breathing and Circulation) when attempting CPR.**

Even when performed by an experienced veterinarian, CPR does not always work. Don't be discouraged if your attempt fails, but know that you did try to save an animal's life.

A = Airway

Does the animal have an open airway? (The airway is the passage the animal breathes through. Check to see if the throat and mouth are clear of foreign objects.) If the answer is **YES**, go to *Breathing.* If the answer is **NO**, you need to open the airway. Do the following:

1. Lay the animal down, on either side.
2. Gently tilt the head slightly back to extend the neck and head.

Step 2

3. Pull the tongue between the front teeth.

4. Use your finger to check for and remove any foreign material or vomit from the mouth.

Step 3

Do not place your fingers inside the mouth of a conscious animal—you may be bitten!

B = Breathing

Is the animal breathing? If the answer is **YES**, allow the animal to assume the body position most comfortable for them. Then, move on to *Circulation*. If the answer is **NO**, do the following:

1. Open the airway. (See *A = Airway*, page 15.)

2. For medium and large dogs, seal the mouth and lips by placing your hands around the lips, gently holding the muzzle closed. For cats and small dogs (less than 30 pounds), your mouth will seal the mouth and lips.

Step 2

3. Place your mouth over the animal's nose and forcefully exhale.

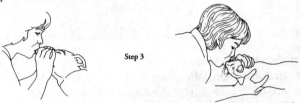

Step 3

4. Give four or five breaths rapidly, then check to see if your pet is breathing without assistance. If the animal begins to breathe, but the breathing is shallow and irregular, or if breathing does not begin, continue artificial respiration until you reach the veterinary hospital or for a maximum of 20 minutes. (Beyond 20 minutes there is little chance of reviving your pet.)

Do not attempt this on a conscious animal

Use the following breathing rates:

- Small dog (under 30 pounds) or cat: 20–30 breaths per minute.
- Medium or large dog (over 30 pounds): 20 breaths per minute.

C = Circulation

Is there a heartbeat or a pulse? If the answer is **NO**, perform chest compressions. Do the following:

Small Dog (Under 30 Pounds) or Cat

1. Lay your pet down, on the animal's right side.
2. Kneel next to your pet with the animal's chest facing you.

3. Place the palm of one of your hands over the ribs at the point where the elbow touches the chest. Place your other hand underneath the right side of the animal. (See *Heart Rate and Pulses,* page 10.)

4. Compress the chest ½–1 inch (your elbows should be softly locked during compressions).

5. Chest compressions are alternated with breaths.

6. If working alone, do five compressions for each breath, then check for a pulse.

7. If there are two people, one person does the breathing while the other does the compressions at a rate of three compressions for each breath, then check for a pulse.

Medium to Large Dog (30 to 90 Pounds)

1. Stand or kneel with the animal's back towards you.

2. Extend your arms at the elbows.

3. Cup your hands over each other.

4. Compress the chest at the point where the left elbow lies when pulled back to the chest. (See *Heart Rate and Pulses,* page 10.)

5. Compress so the chest moves about 1–3 inches with each compression.

6. If working alone, do five compressions for each breath, then check for a pulse.

7. If there are two people, one person does the breathing while the other performs the compressions at a rate of two or three compressions for each breath, then check for a pulse.

Giant Dogs (Over 90 Pounds)

1. Use technique for medium and large dogs.

2. If working alone, do ten compressions for each breath, then check for a pulse.

3. If there are two people, one does the breathing, while the other performs the compressions at a rate of six compressions for each breath, then check for a pulse.

Do not assume there is no heartbeat or pulse simply because an animal is not breathing. Do not start chest compressions before checking for a heartbeat. (If the animal is conscious and responds to you, then the heart is beating).

Continue CPR until the animal has a strong heartbeat and pulse, or until you reach the veterinary hospital, or until 20 minutes have passed and your efforts have not been successful.

CPR can be performed on the way to the veterinary hospital, as long as there are at least two people present (one to drive).

SHOCK

Shock is a body's response to a change in blood flow and oxygen to the internal organs. This can occur as a result of a sudden loss of blood, a traumatic injury, heart failure, severe allergic reaction (anaphylactic shock), organ disease or an infection circulating through the body (septic shock). There are three stages of shock, which may look very different:

Early Shock

The body attempts to compensate for the decreased flow of fluids and oxygen to the tissues.

Signs
- Increased heart rate (see *Normal Heart and Pulse Rates,* page 12).
- Normal to increased intensity of pulses (may feel like they are "pounding").
- Mucous membranes may look redder than normal (this is common with septic shock).
- Capillary refill time of one to two seconds (see *Capillary Refill Time,* page 14).
- Body temperature may be low or, in the case of septic shock, may be elevated.

Middle Stages of Shock

The body begins to have difficulty compensating for the lack of blood flow and oxygen.

Signs
- Hypothermia (low body temperature). Hairless areas may feel cool to the touch (see *Normal Temperatures,* page 13).
- Weak pulse.
- Capillary refill time is prolonged (see *Capillary Refill Time,* page 14).
- Heart rate is increased (see *Normal Heart and Pulse Rates,* page 12).
- Mucous membranes are pale.
- Depressed mental state.
- Cool limbs.

End Stage or Terminal Shock

Occurs when the body can no longer compensate for the lack of oxygen and blood flow to its vital organs.

Signs

- Slow respiratory rate. See *Normal Breathing Rates,* page 12.
- Slow heart rate. See *Normal Heart and Pulse Rates,* page 12.
- Depressed mental state or unconsciousness.
- Prolonged capillary refill time. See *Capillary Refill Time,* page 14.
- Weak or absent pulse.

Cardiopulmonary arrest may soon follow! Prepare to administer CPR. An animal who is in shock, or who you suspect is in shock, should be taken to a veterinary hospital immediately.

First Aid

1. Assess the ABCs of CPR and administer as needed. See *CPR,* page 15.
2. Control bleeding that may be occurring. See *Bleeding,* page 21.
3. Warm the animal by using a thermal blanket. See *First Aid Kit,* page 89. Wrap the blanket around the animal's body.
4. Elevate the hind end slightly by placing a blanket underneath the hind end. Note: do not do this if you suspect a broken back. See *Back, Broken,* page 26.
5. Transport to a veterinary hospital immediately.

CHOKING

Causes

- Food, toy or other object stuck in the throat
- Ill animal choking on their own vomit
- Trauma to the neck or throat region
- Upper respiratory disease
- Tongue swelling due to an allergic reaction

Signs

- Animal stops breathing
- Struggling or gasping to breathe
- Loud breathing sounds
- Anxiousness
- Gums may be blue or white
- History of chewing or playing with objects such as rawhides and balls

First Aid

Use caution not to get bitten, especially if you must work on a conscious or semi-conscious animal.

Step 1

1. Open the mouth and carefully sweep from side to side with your finger to see if you can feel and dislodge the object. Be careful not to push the object further into the throat or to get bitten.

Step 2

2. Pull the tongue forward, removing any object, vomit or foreign material present.

3. If the animal is small enough for you to comfortably lift and suspend, suspend the animal by the hips with the head hanging down.

Step 3

4. If the animal is too large to suspend, hold the animal's hind legs in the air (like a wheelbarrow) so the head hangs down.

Step 4

5. If the object does not come out by doing this, perform the following:

- Have the animal either stand or lie down.

- Place your arms around the animal's waist.

- Close your hands together to make a fist and place the fist just behind the last rib.

- Compress the abdomen by pushing up with this fist five times in a quick and rapid manner. (This is similar to the Heimlich maneuver commonly performed on humans to dislodge materials in the throat.)

Step 5

- Perform rescue breathing for five breaths. See *B = Breathing*, page 16. Even a small amount of air getting past the foreign object will make this thrust maneuver more effective.

Step 5

6. If this is not successful in dislodging the object, administer a "sharp blow" with the flat side of your hand between the shoulder blades, then repeat the abdominal compressions.

Step 6

7. Carefully sweep the mouth with your finger, to see if you can dislodge the object, if it has not come out on its own.

Once the object is dislodged, stop the thrusts, check for the ABCs, initiate CPR if needed and get the animal to a veterinary hospital at once. See *CPR*, page 15.

Do not attempt to place fingers in the mouth of an animal who is growling.

BLEEDING

If the wound is rhythmically spurting blood, this may indicate a bleeding artery. Arterial bleeding is more difficult to stop, bleeds more rapidly and causes a much greater loss of blood than bleeding of a vein. Slower oozing of blood indicates bleeding of a vein, which is much easier to stop and less dangerous. (For nose bleeds, see *Nose Bleeds,* page 68. For bleeding ear flaps, see *Ear Problems,* page 50.)

First Aid

1. Wearing latex gloves, hold a piece of gauze, wash cloth or other clean material over the bleeding site and apply direct pressure. If the material becomes soaked through, do not remove it (you may disturb a clot—which is the body's attempt to stop bleeding) but apply another cloth over it. Do this repeatedly if necessary. Direct pressure is the safest way to stop bleeding until you can reach a veterinary hospital.

Step 1

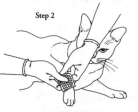
Step 2

2. If bleeding has not stopped and blood is spurting, in addition to direct pressure over the wound, hold the area just *above* the wound with your hand. (You are attempting to close off the blood vessel to the area.) If the blood is flowing heavily but not spurting, hold the area just *below* where it is bleeding to close off the blood vessels.

3. If holding above or below the wound fails to stop the bleeding, apply a pressure bandage.

Step 3

- Wrap gauze or other soft material around the wound just tight enough to stop the bleeding.

- Secure with tape.

- Do not make it too tight. If you are working on a limb, check repeatedly for swelling of the toes or toes that become cold; these indicate your bandage is too tight, in which case you will need to loosen it.

4. If the limb does not appear to be broken, elevate the limb above the level of the heart, while continuing to apply direct pressure.

5. If none of the above techniques works, resort to applying hand pressure to pressure points.

Pressure Point Technique

Pressure points are areas from which the blood vessels travel; if you apply hand pressure to them, the bleeding should stop.

To use the pressure point technique, apply firm, even pressure to the appropriate pressure point:

- *Bleeding on the front limbs.* Place three fingers up and into the armpit on the side with the bleeding limb.

- *Bleeding on the back limbs.* Place three fingers to the area of the inner thigh where the leg meets the body wall, on the side with the bleeding limb.

- *Bleeding of the head.* Place three fingers at the base of the lower jaw (the angle just below the ear) on the same side and below where the bleeding is occurring.

- *Bleeding of the neck.* Place three fingers in the soft groove next to the wind pipe (which feels round and hard) on the side of the neck where the bleeding is occurring, just below the wound. Be sure not to apply pressure to the wind pipe itself.

When using pressure points to control bleeding, you must release pressure slightly, for a few seconds, at least every ten minutes. This helps prevent permanent damage.

Avoid using the neck pressure point on any animal suspected of having a head injury, unless you feel the animal's life is in immediate danger. Ensure you do not restrict breathing.

Tourniquet Technique

Use only on limbs—never place a tourniquet around the neck! **This technique can cause a lot of damage and should only be used as a last resort, for a life or death situation. (For example, the animal has lost enough blood to lose consciousness.)**

1. Wrap a wide strip of cloth or gauze (about 2 inches) twice around the limb above the area that is bleeding.

2. *Do not make a knot.*

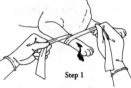
Step 1

3. Tighten the gauze or cloth by wrapping each end of the cloth around a rigid object such as a stick.

4. Turn the stick slowly and just enough to stop blood flow. Write the time on a piece of tape on the tourniquet so you can keep track.

Step 3

Step 4

5. Loosen the tie for several seconds at least every 10 minutes to help avoid permanent tissue damage.

6. Be aware this animal may lose the limb due to the interrupted blood supply.

Pressure points and tourniquets should be used only as a last resort to stop bleeding in a life and death situation, as persistent decreased blood flow to the area may cause severe damage.

COMMON EMERGENCIES AND PROBLEMS REQUIRING IMMEDIATE ATTENTION

ABRASIONS

Abrasions are scrapes to the top layers of the skin.

Cause
- Injury

Signs
- Scrape in the skin
- Oozing of blood
- Redness

First Aid
1. Wash your hands and wear latex gloves if possible.

2. Apply sterile, water-soluble lubricant (see *First Aid Kit*, page 89) to the area. This is done so hair does not contaminate the wound while you shave the area.

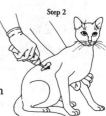
Step 2

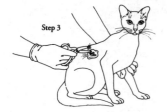
Step 3

3. Clip hair around area gently with grooming clippers, a razor or scissors. If using scissors, do not get too close to the skin and keep scissors parallel to the skin. That way, if the animal moves suddenly you're less likely to poke or cut the skin.

4. Flush the wound with warm water or saline solution (add one teaspoon of salt to a quart of warm water). Flush the wound by pouring the water or saline solution over the wound. The goal of flushing is to remove the lubricant you placed there.

Step 4

5. Wash the wound with water or saline solution to remove any dirt or debris from the wound surface.

If the abrasion is larger than a quarter, seems painful, does not seem to heal or you are not certain how deep or how severe the abrasion is, take your pet to the veterinary hospital.

ALLERGIC REACTIONS

Insect Bites

Causes
- Bee stings and spider bites are most common in dogs and cats during the warmer months.
- Insects often sting the soft, less hairy areas of your pet, such as the nose and feet.

Signs
- Pain, itching, licking at site of sting.
- Swelling of sting site, which may spread and include the face and neck.
- Hives around the site or spreading to other parts of the body (hives look like bumps in the skin).
- Redness at the sting site.
- Vomiting or diarrhea.
- Breathing difficulty.
- Shock. This is referred to as *anaphylactic shock*, a severe form of allergic reaction which may occur immediately or progressively over several hours . (See *Shock*, page 18.)

First Aid
1. If the face and neck are swollen, check the ABCs of CPR. If your pet cannot breathe, initiate rescue breathing. See *CPR*, page 15.
2. Check for signs of shock. See *Shock*, page 18.
3. Check the area to see if stinger is still present. The stinger is very small and often black in color. If you find it, brush it off with a firm object, such as your fingernail or a credit card. Do not attempt to pick it out like an ordinary splinter, as this may cause more release of toxin.
4. Apply a paste of baking soda and water.
5. Apply cold or ice packs, wrapped in a towel, to the swollen area.
6. Transport to a veterinary hospital.
7. It may be appropriate to give the animal the over-the-counter antihistamine Diphenhydramine, if you have spoken to your veterinarian in advance and have received approval.

Doses: Diphenhydramine

- Small dogs and cats (less than 30 pounds): 10 mg.
- Medium dogs (30–50 pounds): 25 mg.
- Large dogs (greater than 50 pounds): 50 mg.

Only give oral medication if your pet is conscious, able to breathe and not vomiting! Only give the antihistamine if you have spoken to your veterinarian in advance.

Skin Allergies

Causes
- Flea and tick products
- Grooming aids
- Shampoos
- Grass or other plants
- Household cleaning products
- Flea bites

Signs
- Red skin
- Itchiness
- Hives
- Swelling

First Aid
1. Wash the animal thoroughly using a very mild soap such as baby shampoo.
2. Apply cold compresses to the affected area.
3. Apply a baking soda and water paste.
4. Administer Diphenhydramine, if this has previously been approved by your veterinarian. See *Doses: Diphenhydramine,* page 25.

BALANCE, LOSS OF

Causes
- Inner ear infection
- Foreign object in the ear
- Brain disease
- Problem with the balance center in the brain (called *peripheral vestibular disease*)
- Parasitic disease

Signs

- Falling to one side
- Head tilting to one side
- Vomiting
- Circling in one direction
- Eyes appear to move side to side or up and down rapidly
- Drooling

First Aid

1. Any animal with these symptoms should be examined by a veterinarian as soon as possible.
2. Look inside the animal's ears. If they are red, swollen or contain a lot of debris, the animal may have an ear infection. Take the animal to a veterinarian for treatment.

Prolonged, untreated ear infections can lead to hearing loss or brain infections.

If the problem turns out to be peripheral vestibular disease, this is a disease whose cause is unknown, but it tends to occur more often in the warmer months. It occurs in cats of all ages, but more commonly in older rather than younger dogs. Peripheral vestibular disease generally clears up, on its own, in 2–3 weeks.

If you suspect peripheral vestibular disease, or if your pet has any of the signs of the disease, the animal must be examined by a veterinarian to rule out more serious brain diseases. If the veterinarian diagnoses peripheral vestibular disease, it is vital you keep your pet out of danger and away from staircases, balconies and open windows. Do not allow your pet to roam outdoors.

BACK, BROKEN

Causes

- Severe traumatic injury
- Animal abuse

Signs

- Animal unable to move the hind legs or both front and hind legs
- May dribble urine or feces
- Anus is open
- May see a "divot"(an area on the spine that appears lower than the rest of the back)

- Pain
- Front legs may be stiff and extended

TIP: *Keeping your pet indoors or under your control outdoors is the best way to protect against most accidents.*

First Aid

1. Check the ABCs of CPR; administer CPR as needed. See *CPR,* page 15.
2. Try to slide a board under the animal, keeping the animal as still as possible:

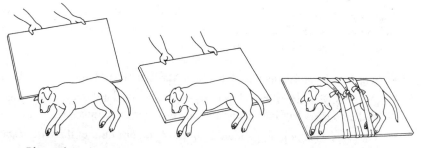

- Place a board on its side along the back of the animal.
- It is best if the head, chest and legs can be held to prevent movement.
- Lower the board and, at the same time, slide the animal onto it, keeping the body and head as still as possible.
- Secure the animal to the board by placing tape or torn strips of cloth over the animal and around the board.
- Transport to a veterinary hospital immediately.

Be careful of stray animals who seem to be unable to use some or all of their limbs, as this may be a sign of rabies infection.

BIRTHING EMERGENCIES

It is best for pets to be spayed or neutered; it makes them healthier and happier. You may, however, take in a stray or otherwise acquire an animal who is pregnant. If you suspect pregnancy, take the dog or cat to your veterinarian for advice and treatment. Once you know the animal is pregnant, prepare in advance by providing a whelping box, bedding and a heat source. If you are faced with an unexpected birth, use the following information as a guide.

In both dogs and cats, normal pregnancies last 62–64 days. About a day before giving birth the body temperature decreases to less than 100° Fahrenheit, decreased appetite is noticed, and nesting behavior (gathering materials for a bed) may get very intense.

Did you know millions of unwanted dogs and cats are taken to animal shelters each year because there aren't enough good homes? Please spay or neuter your pets!

Labor and Delivery

Stage one—the cervix dilates. The animal generally appears nervous or anxious and may pace, pant, lie down and get up a lot; this may last for 6 to 12 hours. Contractions will not be visible.

Stage two—forceful visible uterine contractions occur. She actively strains to expel each puppy or kitten. These contractions look as if she is trying to defecate while lying on her side, and she often is panting.

- Stage two labor usually lasts 3–6 hours. May last 10–12 hours if she is disturbed.
- One puppy or kitten should be born every 4–6 hours if the contractions are weak and every half hour if contractions are strong and forceful.
- The first kitten or puppy should be born within one hour of the start of stage-two labor.
- The placenta should come out with each puppy or kitten, or shortly afterward. (This is referred to as the third stage of labor.)

Normal position of puppies and kittens
Slightly more than half of puppies and kittens are born head first and the rest are born rear-end first. Both positions are normal.

After birth
- Mother should clean off each puppy and kitten after being born.
- The mother should break the cord with her teeth.
- Usually, she will eat the placenta.
- The mother will have a vaginal discharge that is red to brown or dark greenish in color (lochia), which may persist for up to four weeks, but should be small in amount after the first few days. If this discharge appears bright red, or begins to look like pus or have a foul odor, an infection may be present and she needs to be examined by a veterinarian.

Birthing Problems

Causes
- Mother's pelvis is structurally too small for normal deliveries of puppies or kittens
- Puppy or kitten is unusually large; too large for the mother to deliver
- Prior injury to mother's pelvis, for example, a fracture
- Abnormal position of puppy or kitten

- Uterus not contracting strongly enough
- Twisted uterus
- Deformed or dead fetus

Signs

- More than two days past due date (if known) or a dark vaginal discharge with a foul odor.
- Active labor for more than four hours with no puppy or kitten.
- More than a half hour of active continuous straining between puppies or kittens with no puppy or kitten produced. (Active straining is seen as an obvious contraction with the dog or cat trying to push.)
- Kitten or puppy at vulva, but mother unable to push them out within 20 minutes.
- Mother looks weak, sick and depressed.
- Bloody discharge before birth.

It is a good idea to check on the animal, but do not be overly attentive. If the dog or cat is in active labor for four or more hours with no puppy or kitten, or if more than two hours pass between puppies or kittens, or she has any of the above signs, speak to a veterinarian *immediately* for an assessment, and be prepared to get her to a veterinary hospital.

At the veterinary hospital, the attending veterinarian may attempt to treat her with medication to increase the force of contractions. Otherwise, a cesarean section may be performed.

Some dogs and cats will stop labor on their own if they are disturbed.

First Aid

Puppy or Kitten Visible But the Mother Cannot Push Any Further
- Put on latex gloves (preferably sterile).
- Gently grasp the puppy or kitten with a clean towel (towel not shown) and help to pull the puppy or kitten only when she is bearing down (during an active contraction). *Do not pull a puppy or kitten when the mother is not pushing.*
- The pull should be gentle, backward (out of the vulva and towards you) and in a slightly downward direction.

Mother Not Cleaning Puppy or Kitten

- Allow the mother to try to clean the puppy or kitten. If she doesn't, remove the baby from the sac and wipe the puppy or kitten with a clean cloth, cleaning the mouth, nose (to remove any fluid) and eyes. Rub gently (but vigorously) to stimulate the puppy or kitten to breathe. Then dry the puppy or kitten with a cloth.

- Cut the cord, but only after the puppy or kitten is breathing and pink.

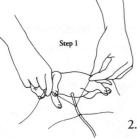

Step 1

1. Tie a piece of fishing line or other heavy string snugly around the cord about one inch from the body, then a second tie about a half inch from the first. (Do not pull on the cord or a hernia may result.)

2. Cut between the two ties.

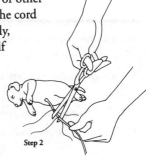

Step 2

Puppy or Kitten Not Breathing

1. Wipe with a towel. Clear the face, nose, eyes and mouth.

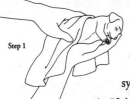

Step 1

2. Hold the puppy or kitten firmly in your hand, pointing the head downwards towards the floor.

3. Clean away fluid from the nose and mouth. (You can suction gently with a baby dosing syringe or bulb syringe.)

Step 3

4. If the newborn is still not breathing, perform rescue breathing. See *CPR*, page 15. You do not have to seal off the mouth when performing rescue breathing, because the newborn should be small enough for you to put your mouth over both the mouth and nose.

5. Repeat vigorous rubbing with a towel, holding the puppy or kitten on a slight downward slant to remove any fluids. Continue to administer rescue breathing as needed. See *CPR*, page 15. Do not over shake or jostle the newborn.

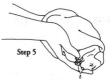

Step 5

If you suspect a problem, call your veterinarian!

BLOAT AND TORSION

Bloat and torsion most commonly occurs in large and giant dogs. Gastric dilation or bloat is a condition in which the stomach fills up with air or food. Torsion or volvulus is a continuation of this condition in which the stomach turns around itself, often misplacing the spleen with it. This cuts off the blood supply to both organs, resulting in life-threatening shock.

Causes
Bloat and torsion are thought to be associated with eating large meals, exercising just before or after eating and gorging on large amounts of food or water. *This condition is a medical emergency!*

Signs
The signs of bloat often occur within hours after a meal.

- Drooling or salivation
- Restlessness and pacing
- Nonproductive retching or vomiting
- Enlargement of the stomach area
- Shock

First Aid
1. Check the ABCs of CPR; administer CPR as needed. See *CPR*, page 15.
2. Check for signs of shock. See *Shock*, page 18.
3. *Transport immediately to a veterinary hospital.*

The animal needs to have his or her stomach decompressed, be assessed for stomach rotation and have anti-shock therapy immediately. *Emergency surgery may be necessary.*

Prevention
Although there are no fool-proof ways to prevent bloat, some things may help:

- Feed your pet more than once daily. Two meals of equal size are best.
- Do not allow your pet to exercise directly before or after a meal; separate by at least one hour.
- Do not allow your pets access to bulk food sources from which they might gorge themselves.
- Don't allow your dog to drink large volumes of water at one time, particularly right after exercise.

BLOOD CALCIUM, LOW AFTER BIRTH (ECLAMPSIA)

Eclampsia may occur in female cats and dogs late in pregnancy to a few weeks after giving birth.

Causes
- Most common in small or toy breeds of dogs; occasionally occurs in cats
- Usually seen two to four weeks after giving birth
- Caused by low levels of calcium in the blood

Signs
- Muscle tremors which may involve whole body, including the limbs
- Seizures
- Fever

First Aid
1. *You must transport your pet to a veterinary hospital immediately.*
2. Puppies or kittens should stop nursing after this occurs. They must, therefore, be given a supplemental formula. Ask your veterinarian for instructions on how to do this.

Prevention
- Feed the mother puppy food or kitten food two to three weeks before delivery and continue this for four weeks after delivery.
- Have your dog or cat spayed.

Blood in Urine

Causes
- Infection (bacterial, fungal or parasitic)
- Inflammation (due to stones or crystals in the bladder)
- Tumor
- Prostate disease (especially in non-neutered males)
- Uterine infection in a female
- Kidney infection
- Trauma
- Heat cycle (estrus in a female)
- Bleeding disorder

Sign
- Red color to urine

First Aid
1. Watch carefully to be sure your pet is urinating.
2. Check for other signs, such as vomiting, not eating or lethargy.

3. In the case of a non-spayed female, look at her vulva to see if there is a discharge. A small amount of blood-tinged urine is normal for a dog "in heat," but if the discharge looks and smells like pus, she may have a uterine infection known as a pyometra. See *Vaginal Discharge and Uterine Infection,* page 84.

4. Take the animal to a veterinarian. If possible, bring a clean urine specimen from the animal. In the case of dogs, catch a specimen by placing a clean shallow cup, such as a margarine tub or aluminum foil pie plate, in the urine stream. With cats, place a nonabsorbent material (such as fish-tank gravel) in the litter box instead of litter. After the cat urinates, pour the urine out of the box and into a clean container. It is best to get the specimen the same day you go to the veterinarian, but if this is not possible, you can place the specimen in the refrigerator overnight. If you cannot obtain your dog's urine specimen at home, then prevent your dog from urinating outside for at least one hour prior to the veterinary visit so the veterinarian can get a sample.

Prevention

• Neutering of your male pets will help limit the risk of prostate disease.

• Spaying of your female pets will prevent uterine infections.

• In the case of urinary tract infections, you can help prevent future infections by administering your pet's antibiotics as prescribed. Also, adhere to any special diet or other medication prescribed by your veterinarian.

BLOOD SUGAR EMERGENCIES

Diabetes Mellitus

Diabetes mellitus is due to an abnormal secretion or metabolism of insulin, resulting in blood sugar that is too high. Most diabetic pets require insulin injections once or twice daily, although some may be regulated through oral medications or diet alone.

Emergencies can arise if a diabetic pet has a blood sugar level that is too low (hypoglycemia) or too high (hyperglycemia). Diabetes is not the only cause of high or low blood sugar.

Hypoglycemia

Blood sugar level is too low.

Causes

• Overdose of insulin, which can be caused by the wrong insulin syringe being used, a change in the type of insulin used or improper administration

• Reduced need for insulin (sometimes cats will only be temporarily diabetic)

- Loss of appetite
- Liver disease
- Severe infection
- Tumor that secretes insulin
- Poor nutrition in very young animals
- Vomiting up a meal after receiving an insulin injection

Signs

- Weakness
- Wobbly, drunken-looking gait
- Seizures
- Shaking
- Disorientation
- Coma or unconsciousness

First Aid

1. Check the ABCs of CPR; administer CPR as needed. See *CPR,* page 15.

2. Rub corn syrup on the gums, but do not force it into the mouth. Do this even if your pet is comatose. An oral glucose paste is sold at pharmacies; if you know your pet is diabetic or has a history of low blood sugar, keep this product in your house and in your first aid kit.

3. If you do not have the glucose paste or corn syrup, rub sugar water on the gums.

4. Take the animal to a veterinary hospital immediately.

Hyperglycemia

Blood sugar level is too high.

Causes

- Diabetic pet not adequately regulated on insulin
- Insulin not properly administered
- Improper insulin dose used
- Increased insulin demand
- Pet finds a bulk food source and gorges
- Organ disease
- Stress
- Glandular disease

Signs

- Vomiting
- Sweet smell to breath
- Dehydration
- Loss of appetite
- Weakness
- Increased breathing rate
- Change in behavior
- Shock and death can ensue if untreated

First Aid

1. Check the ABCs of CPR; administer CPR as needed. See *CPR*, page 15.
2. Check for shock. See *Shock*, page 18.
3. The animal must be taken to a veterinary hospital as soon as possible. Take your pet's insulin and syringe with you.

BONE, MUSCLE AND JOINT INJURIES

Sprains and Strains

A sprain is an injury involving a ligament (the tissue that connects bones to bones or bones to muscles). A strain is an injury to a muscle.

Causes

- Over-exertion
- Tripping or falling
- Rough play

Signs

- Swelling
- Limping (not placing the limb down at all or placing less weight on it)
- Pain when the area is touched

TIP: *Not every pet is a natural athlete. After consulting with your veterinarian, find activities your pet enjoys and start an exercise program slowly.*

First Aid

1. Three or four times daily, for 5 to 15 minutes each time, apply either a cold compress (ice pack or chemical cold pack) or warm compresses to the injured area. Alternate warm and cold, using warm for one application, then cold for the next. Place a towel between the compresses and the skin.

2. Restrict exercise. Keep the animal in a small closed confined area; walk on a leash only to defecate and urinate.

If there is no improvement in 24 hours, or if injury worsens, seek veterinary attention. An X-ray will need to be taken to make sure there are no fractures or torn ligaments. *Never give aspirin or any other over-the-counter pain relievers to your pet unless your veterinarian prescribes them. They may be very toxic!*

Fractures

Fractures are breaks in the bone. They may occur singularly, in one part of the bone, or there may be multiple breaks in the bone or multiple bones involved. Fractures can have smooth, clean surfaces or have splinters and fragments. Fractures are assessed for severity based on:

- Location of the fracture
- Whether it is a clean break (there may be chips or splinters present)
- Whether the fracture is straight or at an angle
- Whether a joint is involved
- Whether the growth regions of the bone are affected, in the case of young animals
- Whether the fracture site is closed or open (bone sticking through the skin)

Causes
- Trauma (such as a car accident or fall from a height)
- Rough play
- Dog or cat fight
- Animal abuse
- Bone disease

Signs
- Swelling
- Disfigurement (part of the limb seems to be abnormally positioned)
- Pain
- Lameness (not placing full weight on a limb)
- Possible bruising (which can be difficult to see under the fur)
- Piece of bone sticking through the skin

First Aid
1. Keep your pet as quiet and calm as possible.
2. Check the ABCs of CPR; administer CPR as needed. See *CPR,* page 15.

3. If a piece of bone is protruding from the fracture site:

- Wash the area with water or saline (add one teaspoon of salt to a quart warm water).

- Loosely place a dressing over the wound, extending several inches past the opening. Preferably use a sterile dressing such as a non-stick pad or a gauze sponge, or use any clean piece of cloth.

- Wrap the dressing with tape. Extend the tape several inches past the opening. Make sure you do not disturb the bones or wrap the dressing too tightly.

4. If you cannot transport the animal in a box, carrier or a cage, or otherwise keep the animal completely still, you can try to splint the fracture. Splints are placed to keep the fracture immobilized to prevent further damage. **However, an incorrectly placed splint can cause more harm than good.** To correctly immobilize a fracture, **the joints on top of and below the fracture site must be included in the splint :**

- After washing and dressing the area as discussed in Step 3, splint the limb in the position you find it.

- Place a rigid structure along each side of the fractured limb. You can use rolled-up newspaper, sticks, tongue depressors or pens (for cats and small dogs).

- Hold the splint in place with tape placed at multiple sites surrounding the splint and limb, or with cloth strips, wrapped and tied around the limb and splint at multiple spots. Do not disturb the bones or wrap too tightly.

- If no rigid material is available, the uninjured leg may act as a splint. Tape or tie the uninjured leg to the injured leg, placing a thin layer of cotton or cloth between them, if possible. Make sure your tape or ties are not so tight they cut off circulation. To monitor this, make sure you can always place two fingers between the tape or cloth and the limb.

- For a small dog or cat, place the animal in a small carrier or box.

- If a hip or shoulder is broken, transport the animal to a veterinary hospital immediately, keeping the animal as immobilized as possible on a board (or other rigid structure), box or carrier.

Splinting a limb incorrectly can worsen a fracture. If you feel unsure about splinting a limb, it is better to transport the pet in a box or carrier, or in a fashion that causes the least movement to the animal. Do not attempt to splint if the animal struggles too much or if you can immobilize the animal and transport to a veterinary hospital immediately.

Bone Out of Joint (Luxation)

The two most common joints to become luxated are the elbow and hip.

Causes
- Trauma
- Falling

Signs
- Elbow
  - Elbow bent
  - Lower leg pointed away from or towards the body
  - Animal feels pain when you feel or touch the area
  - Foot does not reach the ground
- Hip
  - Animal feels pain when you feel or touch the area
  - Dislocated hind leg is shorter or longer than the other
  - Foot on dislocated leg does not reach the ground when the animal stands

First Aid
1. Check the ABCs of CPR; administer CPR as needed. See *CPR*, page 15.
2. Check for shock. See *Shock*, page 18.

3. In the case of the elbow, you can attempt to splint the limb in the position found (see *Fractures*, page 36), but only if you cannot immobilize the animal and transport immediately to a veterinary hospital.

4. Transport the animal to a veterinary hospital as soon as possible. The sooner you get the pet to the hospital, the greater the chance the bone can be placed back in the joint without surgery.

BREATHING PROBLEMS OR RESPIRATORY EMERGENCIES

Feline Asthma

Cause
Feline asthma commonly starts in young adult cats. It is thought to be due to allergies.

Signs
- Increased breathing rate, especially when exhaling
- Increased breathing effort
- Open-mouth breathing
- Cyanosis (blue color to mucous membranes)
- Wheezing (a musical sound heard when the cat tries to breathe)
- Cat may grunt when exhaling
- Coughing
- Cat may be completely normal between episodes

First Aid
1. Check the ABCs of CPR; administer CPR as needed. See *CPR*, page 15.
2. *Take the cat to a veterinary hospital immediately.*
3. Limit activity by confining the cat in a box or carrier during transport. Manual restraint can make a cat very uncomfortable.

Prevention
There is no absolute method of prevention, but since feline asthma is thought to be associated with allergies, there are many things you can do to decrease the risk of acute attacks:

- Don't allow anyone to smoke in your cat's environment.
- Decrease or eliminate the use of aerosols in the house, including hair sprays, deodorants and perfumes.
- Use only mild carpet detergents and stay away from carpet powders.

- Avoid pine cleaners.
- Clean litter boxes with mild soap and water only.
- Use dust-free litters.
- Keep cats indoors.

TIP: *Cats kept indoors enjoy longer, healthier lives than cats allowed to roam outside.*

Lung Problems

Causes

- Lung infections such as pneumonia may be caused by bacteria, viruses, fungus and parasites
- Cancer
- Trauma
- Electrical shock
- Inhaled objects or vomit
- Heart disease

Signs

- Increased breathing rate and effort
- Pale or blue mucous membranes
- Head and neck extended forward, elbows pushed out
- Abdomen moves when breathing

First Aid

1. Check the ABCs of CPR; administer CPR as needed. See *CPR,* page 15.
2. Allow the animal to assume the most comfortable position in which to breathe.
3. Transport to the nearest veterinary hospital. Carry your pet, if possible, or use a carrier or box.

Upper Airway Disease or Obstruction

Causes

Upper-airway problems can occur in any breed or type of dog or cat, but is most common in breeds with pushed-in faces, such as bulldogs, pugs, boxers, Persians. In these breeds, or mixes of these breeds, the condition is often associated with:

- Overly narrow nasal passages
- Soft palate (back half of the roof of the mouth) that extends too far in the throat
- Abnormalities of the larynx (area of vocal cords) or pharynx (area behind the nose) that obstruct airflow

- Abnormally small trachea (wind pipe)

Attacks are often brought on by overheating, exercise and stress.

Causes in other types of dogs and in cats may include:

- Paralysis of the larynx. This is most common in larger breed dogs and may be an inborn defect or may be associated with other problems such as low thyroid hormone levels.
- Collapsing trachea. This is most commonly seen in small or toy breeds of dogs; they can be born with it or it can occur later in life.
- Airway tumors.
- Foreign objects.
- Bacterial or viral infections (infectious tracheo-bronchitis, also known as kennel cough).

Signs
- Increased breathing rate.
- Increased breathing effort.
- Pale or blue mucous membrane color.
- A loud, low-pitched sound may be heard when the animal breathes. When loud breathing is noted, it indicates about seventy percent of the animal's airway is obstructed.
- Signs are worsened by stress, exercise and high surrounding temperatures.
- Change in the sound of the animal's voice.
- Unwillingness to exercise or otherwise be active.
- Fainting may occur.
- Coughing, mostly heard in toy dogs with tracheal collapse or kennel cough. The cough sounds like a goose honking. (With kennel cough, spasms of coughing may be followed by retching or gagging.)

First Aid
1. If the dog is experiencing the dry, hacking cough typical of kennel cough, take your pet to the veterinarian for examination and possible medication. If other signs are present, you may need to provide first aid treatment (as in steps 2–5) before taking your pet to the veterinarian.
2. Check the ABCs of CPR; administer CPR as needed. See *CPR*, page 15.
3. Remove your pet from the heat and cool if overheated. See *Heat Stroke or Hyperthermia*, page 63.
4. Keep your pet as calm as possible; if you can carry the animal, do so.
5. Check for a foreign object in the mouth, if you can do so safely. See *Choking*, page 19.

Prevention

- Don't allow your pet to become overheated. Pets can get overheated through excessive excitement or exercise, especially in warm weather. Don't leave your pet in a parked car or outside in the sun without access to shade and cool water.

- Watch your pet's weight. Overweight animals overheat more easily.

- Have your dog vaccinated against kennel cough.

- Surgical correction of anatomical abnormalities, if feasible.

BRUISES

This type of injury may cause serious damage to underlying tissue or blood vessels.

Causes
- Mild blunt trauma
- Bleeding disorder
- Cancer

Signs
- Red marks on the skin
- Swelling
- Hematoma (blood-filled swelling) or seroma (serum-filled swelling) may appear under the skin

First Aid
1. Apply cool compresses to the area four or five times a day for fifteen minutes until the swelling goes down (may take several days for a seroma or hematoma).
2. Bruising can also indicate a clotting problem. If you have any question about the cause of the bruising, take the animal to a veterinarian.

BURNS

Causes
- Jumping on a hot stove (cats)
- Getting too close to an open flame
- Being caught in a house fire
- Animal abuse
- Hot water
- Heating pads or hair dryers
- Chemicals

Burns are classified based on severity: The severity of burn is based upon how deep the burn is and the extent of the body burned. Superficial burns that are extensive can be quite dangerous, as can deep burns that are limited in the area they affect. Severe burns can lead to shock and place the animal at risk for significant infection and possible death.

TIP: *Cats can be trained to stay off of counters and stoves. Use gentle, positive reinforcement.*

Burns involving only the superficial layers of skin

Burns in which the superficial skin layers are affected generally heal well with veterinary care.

Signs
- Reddening of the skin
- Tender or painful to touch
- Swelling

Burns involving deeper layers of the skin

Deep burns usually heal well, although there may be some scarring of the skin.

Signs
- Blisters
- Redness
- Swelling
- Tenderness

Burns involving all layers of the skin, as well as blood vessels

Deep burns involving blood vessels often heal with a lot of scarring. Intensive care and even surgery may be required.

Signs
- Swelling under the skin
- Skin is not sensitive to touch
- Loss of skin

Burns in which the tissues and cells of the skin are destroyed

Severe burns result in severe scarring. Intensive medical and surgical care is required.

Signs
- Area looks charred

First Aid

1. Check for the signs of shock in the case of deep or extensive burns. See *Shock*, page 18.

2. Cool water should be applied as soon as possible. This decreases pain and may decrease the penetration of heat further into the tissues. You can immerse the animal in a cool bath, provided the burn involves only one part of the body

3. If more than one part of the body is affected, do not immerse your pet. Instead, run cold water directly over the areas or place cool compresses on the areas. Immersing an animal with extensive burns may cool the skin too quickly and cause shock.

4. Place a sterile non-stick pad or clean moist cloth over the burned area to keep it clean. ***Do not place any ointments, butter or petroleum jelly on burns.***

5. Take the animal to a veterinary hospital immediately.

CAR ACCIDENTS

Causes
- Pet is allowed to roam free and runs in the path of a vehicle
- Pet gets loose from your yard or a leash
- Pet jumps out the window of a car
- Jumping, falling or being thrown from the bed of a pickup truck
- Running over your pet while backing out of the driveway

First Aid

1. If you have witnessed the event, make a mental note of exactly where on the body the animal was hit, whether the animal was simply hit or was driven over and whether the animal was thrown. Often, even in very serious cases, an animal will get up and attempt to walk away. This does not necessarily mean the animal is not severely injured; it is an instinctive response that makes the animal try to escape danger.

2. Approach the scene cautiously. Alert oncoming traffic by waving a cloth. If traffic has not stopped, safely take the animal to the side of the road before continuing. If you do not have time to assess how best to carry the animal, based on the injuries, simply drag the animal by the fur on top of the body, trying to keep the body as still as possible. Otherwise, use the transport techniques in the section *Carrying and Transporting*

Techniques, page 6. Take care not to worsen any obvious fracture or limb displacement.

3. If the animal cannot move or appears to have a spinal injury, place the animal on a flat board for transport. (See *Back, Broken,* page 26.) If you cannot find a board, use a blanket or shirt (slide the animal onto it and have one or two people hold it on each side as stiffly as possible). If the animal cannot move, there may be a broken back or severe internal injuries and the animal may be in shock.

4. Assess and note the following: position of the animal; presence of blood, urine or feces (the veterinarian will need this information when you get to the hospital).

5. Does the animal have an open airway? Is the animal is breathing? If not, is there a heartbeat or pulse? If the answers to any of these are no, see *CPR,* page 15.

6. If alert and standing up, observe whether the animal is limping or favoring one side. Look for blood, open wounds, bruising or limbs hanging in abnormal positions.

7. If the animal is bleeding, see *Bleeding,* page 21.

8. Check for shock (see *Shock,* page 18).

Any dog or cat who is hit by a car should be taken directly to a veterinary hospital. Many internal injuries caused by the trauma may not show up for 48–72 hours after the incident. These can include slow leakage of blood from internal organs, rupture of the urinary bladder or other internal organs and air or blood leaking into the chest cavity. Because the animal's body is attempting to initially compensate for the trauma, early shock may be difficult to identify.

TIP: *To make car travel safer for your pets, use a carrier (especially for cats), or check out the special doggie seat belts and harnesses available at your pet supply store.*

Prevention
• Keep dogs and cats as indoor pets.

• Keep dogs leashed while outdoors.

• Don't transport pets in the back of open pickup trucks unless the animal is confined in a sturdy, well-ventilated carrier which is secured to the truck.

COLLAPSE

Causes
• Disease of the adrenal glands

• Diabetes (see page 33)

• Kidney or liver failure

• Seizures (see *Seizures,* page 75)

• Heart disease (see *Heart Disease and Cardiac Emergencies,* page 62)

- Ruptured tumor of the abdomen

Signs
- Sudden falling over and loss of consciousness
- Extreme (profound) weakness

First Aid
1. Check the ABCs of CPR and administer as needed (see *CPR*, page 15).
2. Take the animal to a veterinary hospital immediately.

CONSTIPATION

Causes
- Foreign object in the intestines
- Dysfunction of the neuro-muscular system of the intestines
- Change in daily routine
- Dirty litter box (in the case of cats)
- Excessive grooming or eating hair
- Dehydration
- Not eating
- Tumors
- Eating something inappropriate

Signs
- No stool for more than one day
- Small amounts of very hard stool
- Crying or straining to defecate in the litter box

First Aid
1. If the animal is still passing stool but it appears to be very firm and the animal is otherwise healthy (normal eating and drinking), try to add ¼ teaspoon of fiber (such as canned pumpkin or bran) to the diet.
2. If adding fiber to the diet does not work, or if your pet has not defecated for more than one day or appears otherwise ill, take the animal to a veterinarian.

 Never use commercially sold enemas made for humans! These may be toxic and deadly to dogs and cats!

CUTS AND TEARS (LACERATIONS)

Lacerations are wounds that cut the skin through to the deeper underlying layers. They may be deep enough to involve underlying veins, arteries, nerves, ligaments, muscles, tendons or even bone.

Causes
- Accidental injury
- Animal abuse
- Animal fights

Signs
- Bleeding. There may be a great deal of bleeding if an artery was torn.
- Open wound. Underlying structures such as ligaments or muscle may be visible.

First Aid
First aid depends on the extent of damage, the degree of bleeding and the cause of the laceration.

- If profuse bleeding is occurring, do not attempt to clean the wound, as you will encourage more bleeding.
   1. Check the ABCs of CPR; administer CPR as needed (see *CPR*, page 15).
   2. Check for shock (see *Shock*, page 18).
   3. Stop the bleeding (see *Bleeding*, page 21).
   4. Even if there is no bleeding, cover the area with a clean cloth.
   5. Transport to a veterinary hospital.
- If not bleeding excessively, clean the wound (see *Abrasions*, page 23).
- If cause is a bite wound, see *Puncture Wounds or Bite Wounds*, page 73.

DIARRHEA

TIP: *A sudden change in diet can lead to stomach upset for your pet.*

Diarrhea is an increase in the amount, fluidity or frequency of bowel movements.

Causes
There are many causes of sudden diarrhea, ranging from the animal having eaten something disagreeable to the first signs of severe illness. A short list of possible causes follows:

- Dietary problems—eating something improper, such as food off the street or human food—are the most common reasons for diarrhea. Other causes in this category include a change in regular diet or intolerance to previously fed food.

- Stress.

- Parasitic infection (most common in puppies and kittens).

- Infectious disease. These can include bacterial infections, viral infections and fungal infections.

- Tumors in the stomach or intestines; cancer in any organ.

- Disease of an organ or organ failure, such as liver disease or pancreatitis (inflammation of the pancreas).

- Glandular disease. This is common in cats with over-active thyroid glands.

- Chronic inflammatory disease. This is a disease in which the walls of the intestines become irritated and nutrients cannot be absorbed.

- Toxin or drug ingestion (see *Poisoning,* page 69).

First Aid

1. If the diarrhea continues for more than 24 hours, or if the animal is very young (under one year), elderly (over 10 years) or otherwise sick, or if vomiting is associated with the diarrhea, the animal should be checked by a veterinarian as soon as possible.

2. If the diarrhea contains blood—either fresh (red stool) or digested (black stool)—have the animal examined by a veterinarian.

3. Check vital signs such as temperature (see *Taking Your Pet's Body Temperature,* page 13), mucous membrane color, (see *Mucous Membrane Color,* page 13), capillary refill time, (see *Capillary Refill Time,* page 14) and check for dehydration (see *How to Detect Dehydration,* page 14). If any of these are abnormal, have the animal examined by a veterinarian.

When taking an animal to the veterinarian because of diarrhea, take a fresh stool specimen, if possible.

4. Take away any possible culprit, such as a new food or a new toy, whose use coincides with the onset of diarrhea.

5. Switch to a high-fiber, low-fat or bland diet. Bland diets can be made at home, using boiled chicken with skin, fat and bones removed, or boiled chopped meat with the fat drained off, and cooked white rice. (This home-made bland diet should be used as a temporary diet only to control diarrhea. It does not contain sufficient nutrients for your pet as a permanent diet.) Special bland or high-fiber (canned or dry) diets can also be purchased from your veterinarian. If diarrhea subsides after two to three days on the bland diet, slowly mix in your pet's regular food and wean back to a normal diet over the course of a week. If attempts to wean to a normal diet don't work and diarrhea resumes, have the animal examined by a veterinarian.

6. As long as there is no vomiting, provide as much water as your pet desires, although the animal should not gulp down too much at one time. In addition, a pediatric oral electrolyte solution (available in the children's sections of your grocery store or pharmacy) is a good source of some of the nutrients lost in the diarrhea. If the animal will drink this solution, this may help to decrease the chance of becoming dehydrated.

Do not withhold water from a dog or cat who only has diarrhea (no vomiting) as this will quickly cause dehydration. For animals who are vomiting, see *Vomiting,* **page 85.**

7. Medications should only be used at the onset of diarrhea. *Check with your veterinarian before giving any medications.* If there is no improvement after one use, your pet appears otherwise ill or is vomiting, or there is any blood in the stool, do not use the medication.

   • Kaolin/pectin at ½–1 milliliter per pound of body weight. (Use dose syringe or dropper.) This can be repeated two to three times per day.

   • **Dogs only:** Bismuth subsalicylate at ½–1 milliliter per pound of body weight, two to three times a day.

Do not give stronger antidiarrheal agents to your pet without having the animal examined by a veterinarian.

DROWNING

Causes

Dogs are generally good swimmers, but both dogs and cats can experience near-drowning due to:

• Boating accident

• Swimming too far out and getting fatigued or a muscle cramp

• Disasters, such as floods

• Falling through thin ice

• Falling into water from which they cannot escape

• Small dog or cat left unattended during a bath in the bathtub

• Animal abuse

• Not being able to exit a swimming pool (if your pets have access to a swimming pool, make sure they know how and where to get out)

TIP: *Taking your pet on a boat? Make sure your pet wears a life preserver made especially for animals and don't leave your animal unattended or without access to shade.*

First Aid

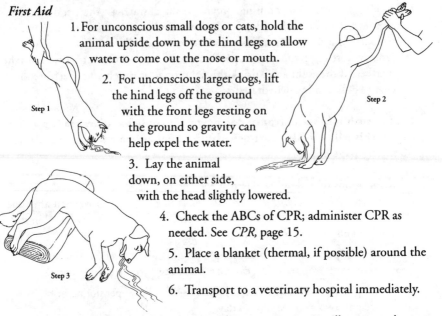

1. For unconscious small dogs or cats, hold the animal upside down by the hind legs to allow water to come out the nose or mouth.

Step 1

Step 2

2. For unconscious larger dogs, lift the hind legs off the ground with the front legs resting on the ground so gravity can help expel the water.

3. Lay the animal down, on either side, with the head slightly lowered.

Step 3

4. Check the ABCs of CPR; administer CPR as needed. See *CPR*, page 15.

5. Place a blanket (thermal, if possible) around the animal.

6. Transport to a veterinary hospital immediately.

Even if you revive the animal, examination by a veterinarian is still necessary because fluid buildup in the lungs, as well as the effects of hypothermia, may result. See *Hypothermia*, page 65.

Ear Problems

Bleeding, Ear Flap

Causes
- Fight with another animal
- Injury

First Aid
- Apply direct pressure to the bleeding site with a cloth or piece of gauze.
- If bleeding absolutely will not stop with pressure alone, a head bandage may be used. Caution must be used to not make this too tight or the animal may have difficulty breathing.

  1. Place a gauze sponge or other piece of clean cloth over the wound.
  2. Wrap the ear with gauze or other soft clean cloth. Hold the ear away from the head, start from the tip of the ear and wrap in a downward fashion.
  3. Once you reach the base of the ear, continue around the side of the head.
  4. Come around the jaw to the other side of the face and head.
  5. Repeat two or three times and tape down the end of your material.

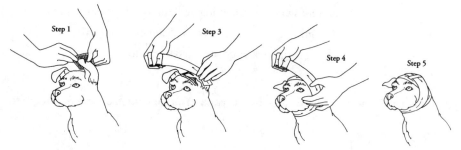

6. Make sure you can place two fingers inside the bandage so it is not too tight.

7. Watch the animal to make sure there are no breathing difficulties.

Ear Infections

Ear infections can vary in severity ranging from superficial infections to deep infections that can cause hearing loss.

Causes

- Infections from bacteria, yeast or parasites.
- Water in the ear (from swimming or bathing).
- Ear mites, a common parasite especially in overcrowded conditions. This parasite is very contagious from and to both cats and dogs.
- Breed predisposition, especially breeds with long floppy ears such as cocker spaniels and basset hounds.

Signs

- Material in the ear (may be black, brown, white or look like pus)
- Bad odor coming from ear
- Itching ear
- Head shaking
- Red swollen ear, with possible blood
- Head tilt

First Aid

Have the animal examined by a veterinarian to determine the cause of the ear infection and prescribe the appropriate medication.

Prevention

- If yeast infections have been diagnosed by a veterinarian, you can help prevent these in the future by cleaning the ear with a mixture of one part white vinegar to ten parts water. Dip a gauze pad into this mixture and clean ears with it weekly. This helps keep the ear pH low, which discourages and prevents yeast from growing.

- Dry your pet's ear after swimming, bathing or cleaning. Use a gauze sponge.

- Keep any animal diagnosed with ear mites away from other animals.

- Keep the animal's ears clean. Ask your veterinarian to show you how to clean the ears safely.

Never place cotton swabs into the ear canal. You may push debris further into the ear.

Swollen Ear Flap (Aural Hematoma)

An aural hematoma is a collection of blood between the layers of the floppy part of a dog's or cat's ear.

Causes
- Chronic head shaking from an ear infection
- Trauma
- Bleeding disorder

Signs
- Swollen ear flap
- Swelling is soft and squeezable
- Infection (see *Ear Infections,* page 51).

First Aid
Take the animal to a veterinarian. This condition generally requires the ear flap to be drained surgically.

Prevention
- Have ear infections treated as soon as they occur.
- If your pet is prone to ear infections, once or twice weekly clean your pet's ears with a veterinary product that breaks up ear wax. (Ask your veterinarian to recommend the best product for your pet.)

Use gauze sponges to clean ears. Never attempt to go deeper into an ear than you can see.

ELECTRIC SHOCK OR ELECTRIC CORD BITES

Causes
Electric shock or electrocution. These injuries occur when dogs or cats bite electric cords. They occur more commonly in cats, puppies and kittens.

Signs

Some signs occur immediately; others may not be obvious for hours or even days.

- Collapse on the floor near an electrical cord.
- Loss of appetite.
- Drooling.
- Foul odor from the mouth.
- Inside the mouth there may be ulcers which can affect the tongue, roof, cheek and gums. Part of the tongue may be missing.
- An electrocuted animal may have difficulty breathing and may cough due to a buildup of fluid in the lungs. Check for shock (see *Shock*, page 18.)

First Aid

Do not attempt to free the animal from the cord if the power is on and the cord is still plugged in.

1. Turn off the power and unplug the cord.
2. Check the ABCs of CPR; administer CPR as needed (see *CPR*, page 15).
3. Check for shock (see *Shock*, page 18).
4. Take to a veterinary hospital immediately.

Prevention

None of these techniques are foolproof, but they may help:

- If you see your pet showing interest in a cord, rub the cord with a hot pepper sauce or other deterrents such as bitter apple (available at pet supply stores).
- Place cords in inaccessible locations whenever possible.
- Unplug all electrical cords when not in use.
- Provide appropriate toys for chewing puppies.
- Use plastic sleeves or cord covers to prevent access to electric cords. These are available at hardware or computer stores.

EYE EMERGENCIES

Any reddened eye should be examined by a veterinarian to make sure no sight-threatening conditions exist.

Cherry Eye

Cherry eye is a swelling and protrusion of the tissue underneath the third eyelid. The third eyelid normally sits underneath the lower lid on the side of the eye near the nose. This condition is more common in young dogs. This condition is not a true sight emergency but must be distinguished from other eye emergencies.

Causes
- Breed predisposition, such as the cocker spaniel
- Eye infection

Signs
- Third eyelid comes up and is visible all the time
- The third eyelid is red and swollen

First Aid
Often this condition will have to be surgically repaired by a veterinarian. Sometimes medication alone will work, but only if the condition is treated early.

Conjunctivitis

Conjunctivitis is a swelling of the pink tissue lining the inside of the eyelids. The conjunctiva can be seen by pulling down the lower eyelid and pulling up the upper eyelid.

Causes
- Infection (bacterial, viral or fungal). This is especially common in young animals and can be contagious to other dogs or cats.
- Allergy.
- Defects in the eyelids (some breeds are predisposed).
- Lack of tear production.
- Chemical irritation.
- Foreign object.

Signs
- Redness
- Swelling
- Discharge (watery, mucus or pus)
- Pain or itchiness

First Aid
Have the animal examined by a veterinarian as soon as possible.

Eye Out of Socket

Causes

These injuries are most often caused by trauma. They can, however, be caused by overly aggressive holding of the neck or pulling of collars, particularly in dogs with small snouts and big eyes, such as the Pekingese.

Sign

One or both eyes bulging out of their sockets

First Aid

1. Administer sterile eye wash or cover the eye with a gauze pad or clean cloth moistened with sterile eye wash, or sterile petroleum-based eye ointment (available in pharmacies), to help keep the eye from drying out while transporting your pet to a veterinary hospital.

2. *Transport the animal as soon as possible to a veterinary hospital.* There is a relatively short window of time to save the eye, so do not delay.

3. Do not place a leash around the animal's neck. Carry your pet, if you are able.

4. Keep the animal from pawing or scratching at the eye.

Foreign Objects In the Eye

Foreign objects are most commonly found on the cornea (the outer layer of the eye) or the conjunctiva (the soft, pink tissues lining all parts of the eye socket and inside the eyelids).

Causes

The most common foreign objects in the eye are pieces of plant material, but there can be many other objects that get lodged in the eye. Normally, objects enter the eye either from flying debris or from brushing against a plant.

TIP: *Dogs who hang their heads out of car windows can be injured by flying debris. Keep your pet safely inside any moving vehicle, and never transport your pet in the back of an open pickup truck.*

Signs

- Swelling
- Redness
- Pawing at an eye
- Squinting
- Runny eyes
- Obvious foreign object

First Aid

1. Gently wash the eye with large amounts of either tap water or sterile saline eye wash. See *Administering Eye Medications,* page 8. Sterile saline eye wash is preferable; it is available at any pharmacy and should be a part of your first aid kit. (See *First Aid Kit,* page 89.)

2. Inspect the eye with a good light source to ensure all of the foreign object is gone.

If you are unable to remove the object with a stream of liquid, if it appears to be perforating the eyeball, or if the eye looks very irritated, take your pet to a veterinary hospital immediately.

Glaucoma

Glaucoma is increased pressure inside the eye caused by a buildup of fluid.

Causes

-   Breed predisposition
-   Displaced eye lens
-   Infections

Signs

-   Redness
-   Squinting
-   Runny eyes
-   Pupil may be enlarged (dilated)
-   Cornea may be cloudy
-   Sensitivity to light
-   Eye may appear enlarged
-   Apparent change in vision
-   Lack of appetite, lethargy, whining, or crying, all of which are symptoms of pain (acute glaucoma may be very painful)
-   Pupils may be unequal in size

The diagnosis of glaucoma must be made by a veterinarian. It involves measuring the pressure of the fluid in the eye with an instrument called a *tonometer.*

First Aid

Acute glaucoma is a medical emergency; take the animal to a veterinary hospital immediately. Your pet will probably have to stay in the hospital to receive topical and intravenous medications to reduce the pressure in the eye in order to save vision. Some animals require surgery to correct glaucoma.

Ulcers, Corneal

Corneal ulcers are defects on the outer layer of the eye.

Causes
- Infection (bacterial, viral or fungal)
- Foreign object
- Scratch, usually from another cat or dog
- Eyelashes that grow inward
- Masses (tumors) on the eyelids
- Decreased tear production

Signs
- Squinting
- Discharge (watery, mucus or pus)
- Swelling
- Pain
- Cloudiness over the eye
- Sensitivity to light

First Aid
Corneal ulcers are extremely serious. If left untreated, they can affect vision, rupture and cause the loss of the eye.

1. Take the animal to a veterinary hospital immediately.
2. Prevent the animal from rubbing the eye. You may want to use a special device called an *Elizabethan collar*. These are available from your veterinarian or pet supply store. It fastens around your pet's neck and extends around the animal's head like a cone. The purpose is to keep the animal from rubbing or scratching the eye.

FALLING (HIGH-RISE SYNDROME)

High-rise syndrome is a condition most commonly occurring in urban settings. It is most common in cats, but can also occur in dogs. Cats will often fall with legs in a down position, with neck and chin towards the ground.

Causes
- Falling or jumping from a window, terrace or other significant height
- Animal abuse

Signs

- Fractures or dislocations of the limbs
- Split lips
- Broken teeth
- Jaw fractures
- Split in the roof of the mouth
- Shock and internal injuries may also occur

First Aid

Often, cats will attempt to run away after the fall (dogs are less apt to do this). This behavior does not mean, however, that they are not seriously injured.

1. Survey the area as you approach.
2. If the animal is not visible, check the entire area around the fall site, including bushes, brush and under cars.
3. Approach the cat or dog cautiously.
4. Check the ABCs of CPR; administer CPR as needed (see *CPR*, page 15). Take particular care when opening the mouth, because a jaw fracture may be present.
5. Control any bleeding. See *Bleeding*, page 21.
6. Check for shock. See *Shock*, page 18.
7. If emergency intervention is not needed on the spot, transport to a veterinary hospital immediately.
8. Your transport technique must take into account the suspected injury. A box or cat carrier to keep the animal in a small enclosed area is best. See *Carrying and Transporting Techniques*, page 6.

Prevention

- Always keep securely fastened screens on open windows.
- Don't allow dogs and cats on terraces or balconies that are not screened, except under close supervision.
- Don't leave windows open wide enough for your pet to squeeze through.

FISH HOOK PENETRATION

The most likely places for fish hooks are around the face and muzzle, inside the mouth and on the paw. It is also possible for a fish hook to be completely swallowed.

Causes

- Dog or cat playing with fishing equipment
- Accidental injury
- Swallowing a baited hook

Signs
- Fish hook protruding from the skin; fishing line protruding from the mouth or anus
- Loss of appetite, painful mouth or excessive drooling

First Aid

The animal should be taken to a veterinarian for hook removal. If it is not possible to get the animal to a veterinarian immediately, try the following:

1. Push the hook through the exit wound until the barb is visible.
2. Cut the barb off with a wire cutter.
3. With the barb removed, pull the hook out backwards, the way it went in.

4. Treat like a wound. See *Puncture Wounds or Bite Wounds,* page 73.
5. Even if you successfully removed the hook, take the animal to a veterinarian for wound assessment and possible antibiotic therapy.

If the hook is embedded inside the mouth, or if fish line is attached to a hook and swallowed, immediately transport the animal to a veterinary hospital. Do not attempt to pull out the hook!

FOREIGN OBJECTS IN THE SKIN

Splinters and thorns are common foreign objects. They can be found anywhere on pets, but are frequently embedded in the pads of their feet. Other foreign objects include porcupine quills, sticks and glass.

Causes
- Accidental injury
- Encounter with a porcupine
- Running into a sharp object such as a stick or fence

Signs
- Not placing any weight, or placing less weight, on a limb
- Swelling at the site of the foreign object

- Licking at the paw
- Obviously protruding quill, thorn or other object

TIP: *Run your hands lightly over your pet's head, body, legs and feet every day to check for foreign bodies, injuries or parasites. Your pet will love the contact!*

First Aid

1. Sterilize a pair of tweezers and a needle, either by passing them through a flame or by dipping them in an alcohol solution.
2. Direct a good source of light at the area.
3. With the ends of the tweezers, take hold of and pull out the object. If it breaks, or if there are deep fragments, particularly of glass, do not attempt to remove them. Take the animal to a veterinary hospital.
4. If the splinter is just below the surface of the skin, try to scrape the overlying skin with the needle, then grasp the object with the tweezers.
5. After removing the object, soak the affected area in a dilute solution of warm (not hot) water and Epsom salts for fifteen minutes. Repeat this three or four times daily until the healing is complete.
6. For cats with a foreign object in the paw, do not use clay litter in the litter box until the wound seals over. (Cats sometimes react to changes in litter by refusing to use the litter box. If this occurs, talk to your veterinarian.)
7. If the wound is deep or if you cannot remove the entire object, or if your pet does not put weight on the limb, take the animal to a veterinary hospital.
8. Also see *Puncture Wounds or Bite Wounds,* page 73.

FROSTBITE

Frostbite is caused by the freezing of a body part or exposed skin, and is a common occurrence in cases of acute hypothermia. The body parts of dogs and cats most susceptible to frostbite include the tail, tips of the ears and the pads of the feet.

Causes

The causes of frostbite are the same as those for hypothermia. See *Hypothermia,* page 65.

Signs

- Discoloration of the frozen area. The skin may be pale or even blue in color initially (in later stages the skin may look black and dead).
- Lack of pain or sensation at the affected area, or it may be very painful, especially when the area starts to warm up.

TIP: *In the winter, clean your dog's feet after a walk to remove road chemicals, salt and ice particles.*

First Aid

1. Take the animal out of the cold.

2. Spray the affected area with warm water.

3. Apply a warm compress to area (ensure it is not hot enough to cause a burn). Do not rub or apply pressure to the area.

4. Transport the animal to the nearest veterinary hospital for care and to assess the affected area to see if there is permanent damage. If the tissue is dead, local amputation may be necessary.

 Any animal with a history of frostbite will be more susceptible in the future.

GUNSHOT WOUNDS

Causes

- Accidental injury
- Animal abuse

First Aid

1. The animal may attempt to run away. Keep the pet as calm as possible.

2. You may see a wound where the bullet penetrated or it may be difficult to find because it is covered by hair. Additionally, there may be a second wound where the bullet exited the body.

3. Any part of the body may be affected, so it is important to examine the animal carefully and thoroughly.

4. Check the ABCs of CPR; administer CPR as needed. See *CPR,* page 15.

5. Stop the bleeding and cover obvious wound sites with gauze, a non-stick dressing or a clean cloth, and hold it in place. See *Bleeding,* page 21.

6. Check for shock. See *Shock,* page 18.

7. If the bullet has penetrated the chest and the animal is not breathing, administer rescue breathing (see *CPR,* page 15) and cover the chest wound with a plastic wrap or, if none is available, gauze or other clean material covered in petroleum jelly (this is an attempt to seal the hole in the chest). These materials can simply be wrapped around the chest. Ensure the wrap is not so tight it constricts chest movement.

8. Transport the animal to a veterinary hospital with as little excess movement as possible.

HEART DISEASE AND CARDIAC EMERGENCIES

Causes
- Cardiac birth defects.

- Improper nutrition. In cats and dogs, lack of, or insufficient amounts of, the amino acids taurine or carnitine can cause cardiac disease (high-quality pet foods contain adequate amounts of these nutrients).

- Enlargement of the walls of the heart.

- Breed predisposition. Certain breeds of dogs and mixes of these breeds are particularly susceptible to some heart problems. For example, toy poodles and other small dogs may have problems with their heart valves and certain large-breed dogs such as Doberman pinchers and boxers are more prone to weakening of the heart muscle.

- Endocrine disorders such as hyperthyroidism in cats and hypothyroidism in dogs.

- Infections such as canine parvovirus and heartworm disease.

- Abnormal heart rhythm.

- Cancer.

 A heartworm can live in the heart of dogs and occasionally cats. The infection is transmitted from one animal to another by mosquitoes. Left untreated, heart-worm infection almost always leads to heart failure, but it's easy to test for and prevent. Ask your veterinarian for more information!

Signs
- Decreased tolerance for exercise.

- Coughing, especially when laying down.

- Bloated belly.

- Increased breathing rate or breathing difficulty.

- Jugular veins (in the neck) may become enlarged.

- Loss of appetite.

- Fainting, particularly following exercise or too much heat. Often the dog or cat will look disoriented or drunk and fall over. This must be distinguished from a seizure. The easiest way is to look at your pet's gum color. If it is white or very pale, it is probably a fainting episode. If the gum color is pink or red it is probably a seizure. Also, during a seizure the dog or cat will tend to be less responsive (and not know who you are).

- Severe pain or inability to move the hind legs. (This rarely occurs in the front legs.) This sign is most common in cats, although it can also occur in dogs. This may occur if a blood clot that formed in the heart becomes lodged in the aorta, where it branches to the hind legs. It can occur in other parts of the body as well. This is an extremely painful condition. Generally the animal will cry out and be paralyzed in the hind legs.

First Aid

1. Check the ABCs of CPR; administer CPR as needed. See *CPR*, page 15.

2. Check for shock. See *Shock*, page 18.

3. In the case of cats who cry out and then appear unable to move their hind legs, check for a pulse in the hind legs (see *Heart Rate and Pulses*, page 10). This pulse will be absent if there is a clot. Also look at the color of the nails of the hind legs. Pink is normal and means there is blood flowing to the area; white or blue indicates blood is not reaching that area. This foot may feel cooler to touch than the unaffected limbs.

4. In the case of dogs, rear-leg collapse is not commonly the result of a cardiac emergency, but begin by following steps 1 and 2. In the more likely case that a dog's rear-end collapse is the result of a slipped disc, see page 77.

5. Take the animal to a veterinary hospital immediately.

Prevention

*   Feed your pet a high quality food.

*   Keep your dog up to date on heartworm testing and preventative medication. Ask your veterinarian if your cat should be tested.

HEAT STROKE OR HYPERTHERMIA

Heat stroke or hyperthermia occurs when an animal gets severely overheated, most commonly in the summer months.

Causes

*   Pet is left in a parked car (the most common reason).

*   Previous episode of heat stroke. Any pet with a history will be more susceptible in the future.

*   Lack of appropriate shelter for an animal outdoors.

*   Animal is not acclimated to the heat.

*   Excessive exercise in hot, humid weather.

*   Underlying disease state, especially heart or lung disease.

*   Breed predispositions. Dogs with short snouts, such as bulldogs, are particularly susceptible to hyperthermia.

*   Prolonged seizures.

*   Heavy-coated dogs in warm climates.

TIP: Never leave your pet in a parked car! *Even with the windows cracked, your pet can quickly suffer heat stroke—and even die.*

Signs

*   Excessive panting or difficulty breathing

- Body temperature 104° Fahrenheit or above (see *Normal Temperatures,* page 13)

- Collapse

- Bloody diarrhea or vomit

- Increased heart rate (see *Normal Heart and Pulse Rates,* page 12)

- Increased respiratory rate (see *Normal Breathing Rates,* page 12)

- Mucous membrane color is redder than normal (see *Mucous Membrane Color,* page 13)

- Capillary refill time is too quick (see *Capillary Refill Times,* page 14)

- Salivation

- Depression, stupor (acting drunk), seizures or coma

TIP: *Dogs and cats don't have sweat glands so they can only dispel heat by panting and through the pads of their feet. Make sure your pets have plenty of cool water and shade during hot weather.*

First Aid

1. Get your pet out of direct heat.

2. Check for shock (see Shock, page 18).

3. Take the animal's temperature (see *Taking Your Pet's Body Temperature,* page 13).

4. Spray the animal with cool water. If using an outdoor hose, run the water for a minute or so to cool if off before spraying your pet. Spray for a minute or two, then retake the temperature.

5. Place water-soaked towels on the head, neck, feet, chest and abdomen.

6. Turn on a fan and point it in the animal's direction.

7. Rub alcohol under the animal's front and back legs or on the pads. Do not use large quantities of alcohol (more than half a pint), as it can be toxic to dogs and cats.

8. Take the animal to the nearest veterinary hospital immediately.

The goal is to decrease the body temperature to about 104° Fahrenheit in the first 10–15 minutes. Once 104° is reached, you must stop the cooling process. Even if you successfully cool your pet down to 104°, you must take the animal to a veterinarian as soon as possible. Many consequences of hyperthermia won't show up for hours or even days. Some of these conditions can be fatal if not treated medically. Potential problems include:

- Kidney failure

- Problems with blood clotting

- Destruction of the digestive tract lining
- Neurologic problems, including seizures and swelling of the brain
- Abnormal heart rhythms
- Respiratory arrest

Hot Spots

Hot spots are inflamed areas on the skin that are aggravated by the animal licking, biting and scratching at the area. These are often found on the legs, but they can occur anywhere on the body. Hot spots vary in severity depending on how long or intensely the animal has been biting or scratching at the area. The lesions start red or pink and hairless owing to the animal's constant biting, and may end up as bleeding, infected areas.

Causes
- The area may have originally been irritated by a sting, an external parasite such as a flea, a foreign object, a scrape or an allergic condition.
- Food allergies.
- Psychological causes, such as boredom.

TIP: *Create an interesting environment for your pet to relieve boredom. Give your cat or dog safe toys, exercise and lots of attention.*

First Aid
1. Shave the area with grooming clippers or a razor.
2. Clean the area with warm water.
3. Look for the presence of any foreign objects, including insect stingers or fleas.
4. You can try a topical over-the-counter antibiotic and steroid cream or ointment, but this generally will not be enough for severe hot spots.
5. You may place an Elizabethan collar on the animal. You can purchase one from your veterinarian or pet supply store. These collars fasten around your pet's neck and extend around the head like a cone. This keeps the animal from biting at most parts of the body.
6. If topical treatments don't work, have the animal examined by a veterinarian.

Hypothermia

Hypothermia is a drastic lowering of the body temperature. The consequences of extreme hypothermia may include neurologic problems (including coma), heart problems, kidney failure and slow or no breathing.

Causes

- Underlying illness.
- Very old and very young animals are sometimes unable to regulate body temperature properly.
- Stray or outdoor animal caught in the cold or a storm without shelter.
- Animal not acclimated to the cold weather.
- Shock.

Signs

- Weak pulse
- Decreased heart rate (see *Normal Heart and Pulse Rates,* page 12)
- Pupils may be dilated (the black inner circle of the eye appears larger)
- Shivering
- Mucous membranes are pale or blue (see *Mucous Membrane Color,* page 13)
- Body temperature is below 95° Fahrenheit (see *Normal Temperatures,* page 13)
- Stupor, unconsciousness or coma

TIP: *Very young or old dogs, and dogs with short-hair, may need a coat or sweater for walks during the coldest months.*

First Aid

1. Remove the animal from the cold.
2. Check the ABCs of CPR; administer CPR as needed. See *CPR,* page 15.
3. Assess for shock. See *Shock,* page 18.
4. Take a rectal temperature. See *Taking Your Pet's Body Temperature,* page 13.
5. Wrap the animal in a blanket. See *First Aid Kit,* page 89.
6. Place warm water bottles next to the animal. Wrap the bottles in towels to prevent burns.
7. Transport to a veterinary hospital.

MAMMARY GLANDS, SWOLLEN OR RED

This condition is called *mastitis.* It may occur in female dogs and cats when they feed their puppies or kittens. Mammary glands are found on the underbelly of a dog or cat, from the front armpits to the back legs.

Causes

- Infection
- Trauma from nursing puppies or kittens
- Dirty living conditions

- Pregnancy
- Tumor

Signs
- Swollen or red mammary gland
- Gland feels hot to the touch
- Discharge from the gland (may look like milk with blood or pus in it)
- Fever

First Aid
1. Clean the nursing environment, including the whelping box, surrounding areas and anything coming in contact with the animal.
2. Place warm compresses on the affected gland every three or four hours for 10–15 minutes.
3. Have the animal examined by a veterinarian.

Prevention
- Keep nursing and living areas clean and dry.
- Spay your dogs and cats to prevent pregnancy.

Female dogs and cats can also develop mammary gland tumors that can become infected. This condition is unrelated to nursing and should be examined by a veterinarian.

NAILS—BROKEN TOENAILS

Causes
- Not trimming toenails on a regular basis
- Injury
- Cutting a toenail too short during trimming

Signs
- Bleeding from toe
- The animal doesn't place as much weight on the leg with the broken toenail

TIP: *Clip only the sharp tips of your pet's nails regularly using a clipper designed for dogs or cats. Your veterinarian can show you how.*

First Aid
Apply direct pressure to the nail with a piece of gauze or a clean cloth for five minutes or apply styptic pencil or styptic powder to the area. These

items should be a part of your first aid kit (see *First Aid Kit,* page 89). If you do not have these items available, try the following:

1. Take a bar of soap and push it into the bleeding nail or apply flour or cornstarch to the area with firm pressure for five minutes.
2. If you are not successful, wrap the paw (see *Pad Wounds,* page 68). After bandaging the paw, transport to a veterinary hospital.

If you are able to stop the bleeding at home, wait one day (to make sure you do not disturb the clot that has formed) then soak the paw in warm water and Epsom salts. Monitor the site for infection, as evidenced by swelling, pain, redness and reluctance to put weight on the paw. If any of these signs appear, take the animal to a veterinarian.

Nose Bleeds

Causes
-   Injury
-   Infection
-   Tumor
-   Bleeding disorder
-   Foreign object

First Aid
1. Apply an ice pack, wrapped in cloth, to the nose.
2. Place steady pressure on the bleeding nostril using a clean cloth or gauze.
3. Keep the animal as quiet and still as possible.

4. If the bleeding does not stop, is the result of anything but simple trauma (such as a thorn in the nose) or there is no obvious reason for the bleeding, take the animal to a veterinarian immediately for an exam. A small amount of blood from one nostril may be an early sign of a tumor.

Pad Wounds

The pads of your pet's feet contain many blood vessels which cause them to bleed a lot when cut. Due to their location and function, they are often injured.

Cause
The most common cause is stepping on a sharp object, such as a thorn or a piece of glass.

Signs

- Bleeding (may be heavy)
- Limping or not putting weight on the limb
- Wound or foreign object in pad

First Aid

1. Remove any obvious foreign object (see *Foreign Objects In the Skin,* page 59).

2. Wash the area with saline solution (add one teaspoon of salt to one quart of warm water) or with warm water alone.

3. Dry the foot.

4. Bandage the foot by placing a strip of adhesive tape on each side of the foot, starting several inches above the wound and extending several inches past the bottom of the foot.

5. Place a non-stick pad or gauze sponge over the wound.

6. Wrap the paw with gauze, starting from the toes and ending just above the ankle or wrist.

7. Pull the ends of the sticky tape over the end of the bandage as far as it will go, with the sticky part twisted to face and adhere to the bandage.

8. Place an elastic bandage over the cotton, working from the toes to the ankle. Do not wrap tightly.

9. Make sure the bandage is not too tight: check for toe swelling and feel the limb just above the bandage for coolness, swelling or pain. If any of these are evident, loosen the bandage.

10. Transport the animal to a veterinary hospital so the wound can be assessed.

POISONING

There are many potential sources of toxins for dogs and cats, including:

- Many plants, both indoor and outdoor.

- Prescription medications, either prescribed for the animal and taken in inappropriate dosage or belonging to someone else in the household and accidentally eaten by the animal.
- Household chemicals, which may include cleaning solutions; antifreeze; rat or mouse bait, ant baits and other pesticides; herbicides; lead-based paint; and potpourri.
- Non-prescription drugs such as acetaminophen, aspirin or ibuprofen.
- Topical products such as flea powders, sprays, shampoos and dips.
- Inhaled toxins such as carbon monoxide.
- Household foods including chocolate and moldy cheese.
- Drugs such as marijuana, cocaine, amphetamines and alcohol.

TIP: *You can now buy antifreeze that's much safer around animals and children who might accidentally ingest it. Look for antifreeze made with propylene glycol (not ethylene glycol, which is poisonous).*

Causes
- Accidental ingestion
- Animal abuse
- Giving improper medication to the animal without understanding the consequences
- Eating food that may be toxic to the animal, such as chocolate or moldy cheese
- Eating garbage

TIP: *Never give your pet any unprescribed medication without consulting a veterinarian. Over-the-counter medications for humans, such as **ibuprofen** and **acetaminophen**, are toxic to pets!*

Signs
Poisons can be eaten, inhaled or absorbed through the skin. The signs of poisoning may occur immediately, within hours or may take days to appear.

- Vomiting or diarrhea (with or without blood or particles of the ingested toxin)
- Seizures or other abnormal mental state or behavior, such as hyperexcitability, trembling, depression, drowsiness or coma
- Salivation (drooling or foaming at the mouth)
- Swollen, red irritated skin or eyes
- Ulcers in the mouth, burned lips, mouth or skin
- Bleeding from anus, mouth or any body cavity

TIP: *Ask your veterinarian about plants that may be poisonous to pets before adding the plants to your home or garden. Assume a plant can be harmful unless you know it is not.*

First Aid

1. Check the ABCs of CPR and administer CPR as needed. See *CPR*, page 15.

2. Check the mucous membrane color (see *Mucous Membrane Color*, page 13). Certain toxins cause specific changes in the color. For instance, acetaminophen intoxication in cats causes brown mucous membrane color and bright red mucous membrane color occurs in cases of carbon monoxide poisoning.

3. Check the capillary refill time (see *Capillary Refill Time*, page 14).

4. Check the animal's mental state, looking for seizures, increased excitement, unsteadiness, depression or coma.

5. Call your veterinarian or veterinary emergency hospital. Have the following information on hand if possible:

   • Exact name of the poison

   • How much the animal ate or was exposed to

   • How long ago exposure or ingestion occurred

   • The animal's vital signs (temperature, heart rate, breathing rate, capillary refill time, and mucous membrane color)

   • Approximate weight of the animal

Your veterinarian may have you call the National Animal Poison Control Center before coming to the hospital. **The phone numbers for the National Animal Poison Control Center are 1-800-548-2423 or 1-900-680-0000.** There are fees associated with services they provide.

At home you will only be able, at best, to assist in ridding the pet's body of the toxin, depending on the type of poison. For specific types of poisoning, follow the first aid instructions in the following sections.

Topical Poisons

1. Call your veterinarian or the National Animal Poison Control Center for information about the specific poison involved.

2. Wash the animal with large volumes of water. If your pet is having a reaction to a flea product, a mild hand soap or baby shampoo can be used. For oil-based toxins (such as petroleum products), use dishwashing liquid. *Call your veterinarian or the National Animal Poison Control Center before wetting the animal, as water may activate some poisons.*

3. If the poison is in the eye, flush the eye with large volumes of water or sterile eye wash. See *Administering Eye Medications*, page 8.

4. If the poison is a powder, you will need to dust or vacuum it off.

Inhaled Poisons

Gases, such as carbon monoxide, can cause poisoning.

1. Take the animal into fresh air as quickly as possible.
2. Administer rescue breathing as needed (see *CPR*, page 15).
3. Check for shock (see *Shock*, page 18).

TIP: *To protect your family, including your pets, install a carbon monoxide detector in your home.*

Ingested Poisons

It may be appropriate to induce vomiting, but *do not induce vomiting until you speak with a veterinarian or the National Animal Poison Control Center.* With some caustic substances it may be appropriate to administer milk, but this needs to be decided on a case by case basis. Let your veterinarian or the poison control center advise you. ***Do not induce vomiting in the following circumstances:***

- The animal is having difficulty breathing.
- The animal is seizuring, depressed or acting unusually excited.
- The animal is unconscious.
- The toxin is suspected or known to be a caustic substance (such as a drain opener), an acid (such as from a battery) or a petroleum-based product.
- The animal's heart rate is very slow (see *Normal Heart and Pulse Rates*, page 12).
- The object eaten was sharp or pointed.
- There is a history of bloat.
- When the poison container says not to do so.

How to Induce Vomiting

If your veterinarian or the National Animal Poison Control Center advises you to induce vomiting, you can give household (three percent) hydrogen peroxide orally, one teaspoon per ten pounds of body weight (see *Administering Medication*, page 7). This can be repeated every 15–20 minutes up to three times, on the way to the veterinary hospital.

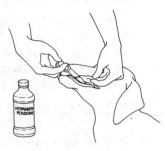

Ipecac syrup can be dangerous to dogs and cats and should not be used to induce vomiting, unless specifically advised by your veterinarian.

If you are not sure what your pet ate, take the vomit to the hospital. If you know what the substance was, take the vomit and the container the toxin was in. *In any case of poisoning, take your pet to the veterinary hospital as soon as possible.*

- If you are unable to induce vomiting, the animal's stomach may need to be pumped.

- If ingestion occurred some time ago and the toxin has already been partially absorbed, efforts at blocking further absorption will need to be made. This may include giving the pet activated charcoal.

- A few toxic substances have antidotes. To determine an antidote, the veterinarian must know what the animal ate.

- Depending on the poison, there may be serious bodily consequences, including organ failure. These consequences must be treated by a veterinarian with intravenous fluids and medications.

PUNCTURE WOUNDS OR BITE WOUNDS

Puncture and bite wounds can look minor from the outside, but can be deceptively deep and serious.

Causes
- Injury from a pointed object
- Bite wound from another animal
- Animal abuse

Signs
- Small wound in skin. If there are two puncture marks, this is a good indication the wound was caused by a bite. See also *Snake Bites,* page 78.
- Bleeding may occur.
- There may be bruising, particularly if the attacking animal is much larger and picks up and shakes the smaller animal. If this occurs, there may also be significant internal injury to both muscles and organs.
- If the wound is not immediately apparent, the injured animal may develop an infection one or two days after being bitten.

Signs of Bite Wound Infection
- Abscess. This is a soft swelling around the wound site that may have ruptured. If so, pus will be visible and may be accompanied by a foul odor. If unruptured, the top of the swelling may be red or blue, painful and the skin looks taut.
- Loss of appetite.
- Fever, usually above 103° Fahrenheit.
- Lethargy.

- Pain when affected area is touched.

TIP: *Neutered dogs and cats are less likely to roam, fight and bite.*

First Aid

1. If the wound is bleeding excessively, control the bleeding (see *Bleeding*, page 21).

2. Check the ABCs of CPR; administer CPR as needed (see *CPR*, page 15).

3. Check for shock (see *Shock*, page 18).

4. Administer basic wound care (see *Abrasions*, page 23).

5. If the cause is a bite wound, it can be extremely serious. Bite wounds often become infected due to the organisms that naturally reside in the mouth, combined with deep penetration by the canine teeth.

   - If you witness the bite, find out the rabies vaccination status of the animal doing the biting.

   - Recheck the rabies vaccination status of the animal that was bitten.

   - If your pet was bitten by a wild animal and the wild animal is dead, take it with you to the veterinarian so it can be sent to a laboratory for a rabies examination. Wear gloves when placing the wild animal in a bag, then seal the bag. If the wild animal is alive, do not attempt to capture it.

   - If your pet is ill and has an abscess that has not ruptured, take the animal to a veterinarian as soon as possible for abscess care.

   - If your pet has an abscess that has ruptured, clean the area as described under *Abrasions*, page 23, and take the animal to a veterinarian.

6. If you suspect a snake bite, see *Snake Bites*, page 78.

ROUNDWORMS

Roundworms is a general term that includes several different types of intestinal worms. These worms may be visible in the stool or they may be vomited up (this is more common in puppies and kittens). Roundworms look like pieces of spaghetti.

Causes

- Puppies and kittens get roundworms directly from their mother's milk when they start to suckle.

- Dogs and cats can pass the worms and eggs in their stool or vomit. Pets can acquire them easily by smelling and eating other animals' feces. It is best to assume that all the pets in a household are infected if one case of roundworms has been positively confirmed.

Signs

- Diarrhea

- Weight loss

- Loss of appetite, or the animal may be very hungry but not gain weight
- Vomiting
- Poor-looking coat of hair
- Bloated abdomen
- You may or may not see actual worms in the stool or vomit
- Anemia (pale gum color)

First Aid

1. Take the animal to a veterinarian along with a sample of the stool. If you see worms in the vomit or stool, make sure the sample includes the worm.

2. Have your pet's stool checked for worms at their yearly physical examination or sooner if you suspect an infestation.

It is very important to treat roundworm infections, as they may be transmitted to humans. Any pet who has been treated for worms should have a follow-up fecal examination to ensure success of the treatment.

Prevention

- Remove your dog's stool after defecation.
- Have your pet's stool checked yearly by a veterinarian.
- Don't introduce a new animal into your household without first having the animal checked and treated for worms.
- Don't allow your dog or cat to eat or sniff feces of other animals.

SEIZURES

Causes

Causes inside the central nervous system include the following:

- Tumor
- Abscess
- Infection within the brain (bacterial, fungal, viral or parasitic)
- Inflammation within the brain
- Malformation of the brain (birth defect)
- Scar tissue in the brain (may occur after a head injury)

Causes outside the central nervous system include the following:

- Organ failure, particularly of the liver and kidney. These organs are the waste treatment plants of the body; when they malfunction, a large buildup of toxic waste products can occur, causing seizures.

- Glandular disease which results in blood sugar that is too low or too high (as may occur in diabetics).

- Poisoning. Many toxins can cause seizures if eaten by dogs and cats, such as some drugs, plants, lead, heavy metals, antifreeze and chocolate.

Seizures can also be caused by epilepsy. The cause of epilepsy is unknown, but some animals have a lower resistance to seizures than is normal.

Signs

- Before a seizure, the animal may seem dazed or anxious, may seek you or seek a safe place.

- Active seizure. The animal will often fall over, twitch, urinate, defecate, drool and will not recognize you. Some seizures may just look like the animal is staring into space or biting at invisible things.

- After a seizure. The animal may be disoriented, walk into walls or appear to be blind. Animals may also behave normally following a seizure.

First Aid

1. Make sure the animal is in a safe place (not on top of a staircase or anywhere from which a fall is possible).

2. Record how long the active phase of the seizure lasts.

3. Keep a log of the animal's seizures. Include the date, time of day, time after a meal and how long the active seizure phase lasts.

4. Keep your hands away from the animal's mouth. Do not attempt to hold the animal's tongue (the animal will not swallow their tongue). Your pet does not know who you are during a seizure and many people get bitten when attempting to handle their seizuring pets.

5. Do not disturb the animal during and after an active seizure.

6. If this is your pet's first seizure, call your veterinarian. This animal should be examined as soon as possible.

7. Seizures lasting more than two minutes or cluster seizures (repeated seizures one after the other) are medical emergencies; these animals are at risk for very high fevers and brain damage. Any animal having cluster seizures must be examined by a veterinarian immediately.

If your pet is placed on anti-seizure medication, it is important to understand that such medication does not cure the cause of the seizure; it simply helps reduce the number or severity of episodes. You must be aware that your pet will probably have future episodes and require frequent veterinary check ups.

SLIPPED DISC (INTERVERTEBRAL DISC DISEASE)

This most commonly occurs in certain small breeds, especially dachshunds, cocker spaniels and poodles, but can occur in any animal. It occurs when a disc (the cushiony material between each of the vertebrae of the spine) becomes damaged and begins to press on the adjacent spinal cord.

Causes
- Breed predisposition
- Injury

Signs
- The animal may initially cry in pain, even without being touched.
- Arched back stance.
- May appear very painful in the back or belly.
- May urinate or defecate without control.
- May not be able to walk at all, rear legs may appear to collapse or may have a lesser degree of paralysis and stumble or drag feet or toes.
- Evidence of trauma.

First Aid
1. Take the animal to a veterinarian as soon as possible. Carry the animal or restrain in a carrier, cage or on a board. (See *Carrying and Transporting Techniques*, page 6.)
2. If complete paralysis occurs, your pet may need surgery to have the best chance of walking again.
3. If there is not complete paralysis, your veterinarian may prescribe anti-inflammatory drugs. Once you give these drugs, you must completely confine your pet; a cage or crate is best. (The anti-inflammatory drugs will make your pet feel better and may encourage more movement than is good for the animal, potentially worsening the condition.)

SMOKE INHALATION

Causes
- Animal caught in a burning structure or grass fire
- Animal abuse

Signs

- Abnormally fast breathing
- Labored breathing
- Breathing may stop
- Singed hair with a smoky odor to the coat
- Coughing
- Discharge from the mouth or nose
- Eye discharge
- Bright red gums in the case of carbon monoxide poisoning

First Aid

1. *Immediately* remove the animal from the smoke.
2. Check the ABCs of CPR; administer CPR as needed (see *CPR*, page 15).
3. Check for shock (see *Shock*, page 18).
4. Transport the animal to a veterinary hospital immediately.

Many of the serious consequences of smoke inhalation may not be apparent for several days. These can be life-threatening and include the following:

- Fluid accumulation in the lungs or chest cavity
- Pneumonia
- Swelling of the mouth and throat
- Body fluid and electrolyte imbalances
- Ulcers or damage to the surface of the eye

SNAKE BITES

Poisonous snakes in the Unites States include:

- **Pit vipers.** These include rattlesnakes, copperheads and cottonmouths. Pit vipers have a depression between their nose and eyes. Their fangs can retract and their heads are triangular in shape.
  - Rattlesnakes can be up to eight feet in length; tails contain a rattle.
  - Copperheads are about four feet long and have no rattles. The top of the head is a rich, coppery orange color.
  - Cottonmouths, also known as water moccasins, can grow to four feet in length. The body is dark and the inside of the mouth is snowy white.
- **Coral snakes.** Fangs are in the rear of the mouth and are not retractable. The snakes can be up to three feet long. They are red, yellow, and black in alternating bands.

Causes
- Curiosity
- Hunger
- Startled or frightened snake

Signs
- Fang marks may or may not be visible, due to dog or cat's hair
- Bleeding puncture wound
- Swelling of the bitten area; can be severe and progress for more than a day
- Pain
- Reddening
- Bruising
- Signs of shock
- Breathing stops
- Blood does not clot
- Neurologic signs such as twitching and drooling

First Aid
1. If you suspect a bite by a poisonous snake, attempt to identify the snake, but don't get close enough to get bitten. If you have to kill the snake to protect yourself or your pet, take it with you for identification. **Be aware that the fangs of a decapitated snake head may be venomous for up to 1½ hours.**
2. Check the ABCs of CPR; administer CPR as needed (see *CPR,* page 15).
3. Check for signs of shock (see *Shock,* page 18).
4. Attempt to keep the animal calm and still. If possible, carry your pet to the car. Any movement may cause the toxin to spread faster.
5. Put on gloves and wash the wound with water and mild soap. *Do not cut open the wound or attempt to suck out the venom! Do not place ice on the area or use a tourniquet!* (Depending on the situation, such actions may do more harm than good.)
6. Immediately transport the animal to a veterinary hospital.
7. Some non-poisonous snakes may also bite. This bite may cause an allergic reaction. If your pet is bitten by a non-poisonous snake, treat as your would a puncture wound (see *Puncture Wounds or Bite Wounds,* page 73) and watch for allergic reactions (see *Allergic Reactions,* page 24). If you are unsure if the snake was poisonous, follow steps 1–6.

SNEEZING

Sneezing in and of itself does not constitute an emergency situation but can be a symptom of problems which need to be addressed. Sneezing may be caused by:

- Upper respiratory tract infection
- Allergy
- Foreign object in the nose
- Tumor
- Bleeding disorder (such as a problem with blood clotting)
- Congenital defect

Sneezing may be accompanied by a nasal discharge which may be clear, look like pus or have blood in it, depending on cause. It is normal for dogs and cats to sneeze periodically, but if sneezing is persistent, excessive or accompanied by nasal discharge, see your veterinarian.

Reverse Sneezing

Dogs (and less often, cats) occasionally have episodes of "reverse sneezing." This looks like the animal suddenly takes in a breath accompanied by a "reverse snort." These may occur several times in a row and they look very dramatic. However, as soon as the reverse sneezing stops, the animal immediately returns to normal. Although the cause is generally unknown, it can be caused by post-nasal drip. Reverse sneezing typically occurs suddenly, as an isolated incident. There is no need to seek veterinary care unless the animal does not return to normal within a few seconds after stopping or seems to be in respiratory distress. If the episode continues, check for shock (see *Shock,* page 18).

TAPEWORMS

Cause
Tapeworms are commonly spread when an animal eats fleas which harbor tapeworm larvae.

Signs
- Round or flat small white worms that look like moving pieces of rice, around the anus or in the stool. These are segments of the tapeworm body.
- For other signs, see *Roundworms,* page 74.

First Aid
1. De-worming medication administered by a veterinarian
2. Flea control

TICKS

Ticks are blood-sucking parasites responsible for the transmission of several diseases to dogs, cats and humans. They commonly jump on animals as they walk through tall grass or brush against leaves, bushes and trees.

Signs
- The tick may appear as a tiny dark colored insect or a fat engorged parasite that has its head burrowed into the animal's skin.
- They may be present anywhere on the body, but are commonly found on the ears (or just inside them) and on the feet or legs.
- The area around the tick may be red and swollen.

TIP: *Ask your veterinarian about diseases transmitted by ticks.*

First Aid
1. If you live in an area that has ticks, or when returning from a park or a hike, check your pet thoroughly. Run your fingers through your pet's entire hair coat; check the paws by lifting each up and inspecting the pads; look between the toes and inside the floppy part of the ear.
2. If you find a tick:
   - Put on latex gloves.
   - Place a small amount of tick spray (available in pet stores or at your veterinary hospital) on a gauze sponge, cotton ball or paper towel and hold it over the tick. This will usually cause the tick to start to back out in 30–60 seconds.
   - When the tick starts to back out, grab the entire tick with a pair of tweezers.
   - Alcohol, mineral oil or petroleum jelly can be used in place of the tick spray, but they generally don't work as well. Don't use matches to singe the tick, as it may burn the animal's skin.
   - Flush the tick down the toilet or, if you are not sure what type of tick it is, you may want to save it in a secure container for identification by your veterinarian. (Different kinds of ticks carry a variety of diseases communicable to animals and humans.)
   - Apply a disinfectant such as alcohol or an antibiotic ointment to the site of the tick bite.

Do not grab the tick and pull without removing the head, or a skin reaction is likely to occur at that site.

If you missed the tick's head, it will commonly look like a small black dot in or just under the skin. This must be removed. You can attempt to remove it as you would a splinter under the surface of the skin, by using a sterilized needle or tweezers (see

Foreign Objects In the Skin, page 59). Otherwise, have a veterinarian remove the tick's head from your pet.

Prevention

There are many products available for prevention of ticks. Before using a tick product, check with your veterinarian to ensure it is safe for your pet's age, species and breed type.

TOXOPLASMOSIS

Toxoplasmosis is caused by a microscopic parasite of cats. The primary risk associated with toxoplasmosis is that it can infect humans. If it infects a pregnant woman during the early months of pregnancy, it can cause serious fetal defects. Humans can become infected by ingesting infective eggs from the soil or by handling litter and not washing their hands before eating, by eating infected animal tissue (meat) or via the placenta in the case of a pregnant women and her fetus. People with suppressed immune systems are also at increased risk for this infection. The most common way that humans become infected is by eating undercooked meat, not by contact with cats.

Causes
• Eating undercooked meat (applies to animals and humans)
• Eating soil contaminated with the eggs
• Eating rodents or other infected prey
• A pregnant cat passing it to her offspring during pregnancy

Signs
• Vomiting or diarrhea

If infection has occurred in other organs, signs can be varied and may include:

• Seizures
• Heart disease
• Eye infections

First Aid
Take to your veterinarian for diagnosis and treatment.

Prevention
1. Good hygiene. Clean litter boxes daily (it takes at least one day for eggs in feces to become infective).
2. Have someone else change the litter box if you are pregnant or have a suppressed immune system.

3. Wear gloves and a mask when cleaning the litter box.

4. Keep your cats indoors to decrease the risk of infection through hunting. Do not allow indoor cats to hunt mice or rats in the house.

5. When gardening, always wear gloves.

6. Discourage stray cats from using your backyard as a litter box.

7. Don't eat raw or undercooked meat or feed it to your pets.

URINARY BLOCKAGE

Urinary blockage can occur in either a dog or cat, but it is most common in adult male cats. If a urinary blockage is left untreated, the body will begin to reabsorb the waste products normally removed by the urine; this buildup quickly becomes toxic. In addition, the bladder may be easily torn after having been stretched for prolonged periods and it may rupture. *If you suspect a urinary blockage, do not attempt to feel the bladder yourself, as it may be very delicate and may rupture from even the most gentle touch!*

Causes
- Urinary stone
- Urinary crystals (most common in male cats)
- Tumor
- Prostate disease
- Chronic bladder disease

Signs
- Crying, particularly when a cat goes into the litter box or when a dog tries to urinate
- Blood in the urine
- Squatting to urinate with nothing or only small drops present
- Frequent, small volume of urine
- Going in and out of the litter box (cat) or crying to be walked frequently (dog)
- Long stays in the litter box
- Urinating outside the litter box or in the house
- Excessive licking of the genital region
- Swelling of the genital region
- Loss of appetite
- Vomiting
- Lethargy
- Slow heart rate

- Depression (hiding, unresponsive or refusing food)
- Coma

First Aid

1. *You must take the animal to a veterinary hospital immediately!* **This is a medical emergency!**
2. If the animal is either a cat or small dog (under 30 pounds), carry the animal by holding the body behind the back legs so you don't place pressure on the bladder. You can also place your pet in a box or carrier.

At the hospital, a catheter will be placed into the bladder to wash it out and allow the animal to urinate. Some animals need surgery to remove the obstruction or stones if they are present.

Prevention

- Finish all antibiotics prescribed for a urinary tract problem, as the condition may persist for long periods even after your pet seems to feel normal.
- Strictly adhere to special diets prescribed for a dog or cat with a history of urinary blockage, bladder infection or stones.

VAGINAL DISCHARGE AND UTERINE INFECTION

Uterine infections may occur in a female pet who is not spayed. They generally occur as she gets older and has gone through many heat cycles. The infections may flare up a couple of weeks to a month after a heat cycle. Infections may rarely occur in females who have been spayed, at the site from which the uterus was removed.

Cause

Bacterial infection, which causes a buildup of pus in the uterus

Signs

- Discharge from vulva. May look bloody or may look like pus and have a foul odor. Some infections have no discharge.
- Loss of appetite.
- Vomiting.
- Licking at vulva area.
- Lethargy.
- Increased drinking and urination.

First Aid

Take your pet to a veterinary hospital immediately. This condition is an emergency and must be dealt with medically and surgically at once, or the uterus may rupture.

Prevention
Spay female dogs and cats to reduce the risk of infection.

VOMITING

TIP: *Never let your cat or dog play with string! Balls of yarn (or any other "toys" that can unravel) are not safe; your pet may accidentally ingest the string or yarn. If you see a string exiting the anus or in the mouth, take the animal to a veterinary hospital as soon as possible. Do not attempt to pull or remove the string, as this may tear the intestines.*

Causes
- The animal eats something improper that upsets the stomach.
- Eating foreign objects. The animal has eaten something that cannot pass through the gastrointestinal tract and is stuck.
- Strings are frequent causes of foreign objects in cats. They often get caught under the tongue, then travel through the stomach and intestines and get caught. They stretch the intestines and can saw through the wall of the intestines.
- Eating toxic materials, including chewing on many types of plants.
- Parasitic infection.
- Glandular disease (commonly seen with hyperthyroid cats).
- Organ inflammation, infection or failure, such as kidney disease or pancreatitis.
- Motion sickness.
- Many illnesses (see *vomiting* in the index).

First Aid
1. No food or water by mouth for 8–12 hours

> *Withholding food and water is only appropriate for young adult or otherwise normal, healthy animals. Elderly (over 10 years), very young (under 1 year) or otherwise ill animals should not go without food or water; these animals should be examined by a veterinarian.*

2. If no vomiting occurs while not eating or drinking, offer the animal a small quantity of ice chips and repeat every two to three hours as long as vomiting does not recur.
3. If no vomiting occurs with ice chips, add a small amount of water (¼ cup for a cat or small dog, ⅓ cup for a medium dog and ½ cup for a large or giant dog) or a pediatric electrolyte oral solution in addition to the water. Repeat every two to three hours if no vomiting occurs.
4. If there is still no vomiting, add a bland or high-fiber diet: two teaspoons at a time for cats and small dogs, one tablespoon at a time for medium sized dogs

and two tablespoons at a time for large and giant dogs (see page 48). Repeat every few hours as long as no vomiting occurs.

5. Over the next 48–72 hours, if no vomiting occurs, mix the animal's regular diet with the bland diet, slowly returning to a normal dietary regime.

6. If vomiting occurs despite withholding food and water, or if vomiting occurs on the reintroduction of food and water, you must take the animal to a veterinarian to rule out more serious and possibly life-threatening conditions and to treat dehydration and nausea.

7. If vomiting is accompanied by other signs of illness, such as fever or lethargy, do not withhold food and water. Take the animal directly to a veterinarian for examination.

Rapid dehydration is possible if the animal is losing body fluids as a result of vomiting, diarrhea and not eating. Dehydration can lead to shock and death. Giving ice cubes or ice chips instead of water can prevent dehydration and keep a cat or dog from drinking too much water too soon.

WOUND WITH OBJECT EMBEDDED

Causes
- Injury from a stick, arrow, knife or similar object
- Animal abuse

First Aid
1. Keep the animal as still as possible.
2. Check the ABCs of CPR; administer CPR as needed. See *CPR*, page 15.
3. Check for signs of shock. See *Shock*, page 18.
4. If the animal is bleeding externally, see *Bleeding*, page 21.
5. Secure the object in the exact position it is in. To secure the object, do either of the following:

- Roll up gauze or any other material that can be tightly rolled and place it around the object to stabilize it in place. Wrap the area with gauze or other available material. Make this wrap snug enough to hold the object in place, but not tight enough to restrict blood flow or breathing.

- Place a brace around the object to hold it still. You can make a brace with tape by shaping it into a ring and fitting it around the object (ensuring you don't jostle or move the object). You can also use something that will fit over the object, such as a foam cup or margarine dish. Cut a hole in the top and slit the side so you can fit the cup or tub around the object without disturbing it.

6. Transport the animal to the hospital immediately. Place in a box or carrier if possible, or transport on a board or other stiff surface. The extent of damage will need to be assessed with diagnostics such as X-rays.

7. If it is not possible to transport the animal to the hospital immediately and the penetrating object is very long, first secure it in place then make it smaller by cutting the object at a distance of five inches from the wound.

Do not attempt to pull out the object. Take care not to jostle or move the penetrating object.

FIRST AID KIT

In this section you find a list of items every pet owner should have at hand for their pet first aid kit. The kit itself can be stored in a waterproof pouch if kept on a boat and in a small tool box or other kind of box in the house. A small version can even be kept in your car trunk. Medications and medical supplies should be kept safely out of the reach of children. Since some of the items in your kit will carry expiration dates, check your kit periodically, discard outdated medications and supplies and make sure you have all the supplies you need. If your pet has any special conditions or needs, ask your veterinarian what additional items you may need for your first aid kit.

Your pet first aid kit should include the following:

- Latex gloves.
- Gauze sponges (available at most pharmacies). A variety of sizes, both large and small, are best to keep on hand.
- Roll gauze, 2-inch width.
- Roll bandages, such as gauze wrap that stretches and clings. These are available at pharmacies, pet stores and through pet catalogs.
- Material to make a splint. This can include pieces of wood, newspaper and sticks.
- Adhesive tape, hypo-allergenic.
- Non-adherent sterile pads. These pads make excellent dressings and can be purchased in most pharmacies.
- Small scissors.
- Grooming clippers (available in pet stores and pet catalogs) or a safety razor.
- Nylon leash (at least one).

- Towel.
- Muzzle. A cage muzzle is ideal, but a soft collapsible one may be more convenient to carry. Get one you already know fits your pet. If you do not want to purchase one, at least have plenty of roll gauze available to use as a make-shift muzzle.
- Compact thermal blanket. These may be purchased in some pharmacies; they are also frequently found in sporting good stores and catalogs. If you cannot get a thermal blanket, have a regular blanket available.
- Pediatric rectal thermometer (may be digital).
- Water-based sterile lubricant (washes off easily).
- Three percent hydrogen peroxide (this will have an expiration date).
- Rubbing alcohol (isopropyl).
- Over-the-counter topical antibiotic ointment.
- Epsom salts.
- Baby dose syringe or eye dropper (non-glass). These are available at pharmacies or in the baby section of most grocery stores.
- Sterile eye lubricant.
- Sterile saline eye wash.
- Diphenhydramine, appropriate dosage for your pet's size, if approved by your veterinarian (see *Doses: Diphenhydramine,* page 25). This will have an expiration date.
- Glucose paste or corn syrup.
- Styptic powder or pencil. Pharmacies carry styptic pencils for use when people cut themselves shaving. Veterinary styptic products are sold at veterinary hospitals, pet supply stores and through catalogs.
- Expired credit card to scrape away stingers.
- A list of emergency telephone numbers including your pet's veterinarian, an after-hours emergency veterinary hospital and the National Animal Poison Control Center (1-800-548-2423 or 1-900-680-0000; see page 71).
- Petroleum jelly.
- Penlight.
- Clean cloth.
- Needle-nose pliers.

How to Have a Healthy, Happy Cat or Dog

Accidents happen. Even if you're a cautious, conscientious pet owner, it's very likely your dog or cat will need first aid care at some point. This book will help you handle emergencies resulting from illness or injury and may even help you prevent some accidents from ever happening.

But what about your pet's everyday health and well-being? That depends on you. It depends on the amount of time you spend with your animal companion, the love and care you provide and the responsibility you take for your pet.

Your relationship with your dog or cat should be a lifetime commitment. And it should bring a lifetime of joy. The following sections can help you make the most out of your relationship with your pet.

Choosing Your Next Pet

- Choosing a pet shouldn't be an impulse decision because it's a choice you may live with for ten or twenty years. Whether you decide on a cat or a dog may start with personal preference, but you also need to consider how much time you have to spend with your pet, where you live, how you live, whether you're financially able to provide necessary care (including veterinary care), whether members of your family have allergies, the ages of any children in the home (younger children require more supervision around animals), who will be primarily responsible for your animal, whether every member of your family wants a pet and whether you already have animals and how they will react to a new dog or cat.

- You need to think about what kind of dog or cat is best for you; it's not enough to choose a pet based on looks. Some pets need more exercise, more grooming, more training—maybe more than you're prepared to provide. Different breeds and types of dogs and cats have very different physical and behavioral traits, some of which may not suit your lifestyle. Do you have your heart set on a purebred or is your heart open to the charms of a mixed-breed dog or cat? Are you prepared for the rigors of a puppy or kitten, or will you welcome an adult animal into your family?

- Cats have the reputation of being "low-maintenance" pets, but even though you don't need to walk them two or three times a day (as you do with most dogs), cats still require a great deal of time, attention, care and companionship.

- When you're ready to add a dog or cat to your life, visit your local animal shelter. Each year, animal shelters around the US receive millions of wonderful mixed-breed and purebred dogs, cats, puppies and kittens who have one thing in common: they all need a good home.

- Once you have chosen a pet, have realistic expectations. Nobody is perfect, not even your dog or cat. Make a commitment to work through behavior and health problems. Don't give up a pet if there is a problem. Instead, seek help from your veterinarian or animal shelter.

MAINTAINING YOUR PET'S HEALTH

- You may adopt your cat or dog from a shelter or from someone who is looking for a new home for their pet. You may rescue a stray or even buy an animal from a responsible breeder. No matter where or how you acquire your pet, your first stop should be to a veterinarian to assess your new pet's health, get advice on training and preventative health care, have a complete exam and receive any necessary vaccinations. Your pet should visit your veterinarian at least yearly, not just for needed vaccinations, but also for heartworm and other parasite tests, a physical examination and a general assessment of your pet's health.

- Keeping your pet's vaccinations up to date is crucial. Puppies and kittens require a series of inoculations. Consult with your veterinarian about what vaccinations your pet will need, as a puppy or kitten or as an adult, and when they are needed, including rabies vaccinations.

PROVIDING DAILY CARE

- To keep your pets at the peak of health, feed them the proper amount and type of food. Choose a well-balanced, name-brand or premium brand dog or cat food that is appropriate for your pet's stage of life. Avoid generic foods—they may not be held to the same rigorous quality standards as name-brand foods. Also remember that dog and cat foods are made differently to account for the different nutritional needs of that species. One common myth is that cats need milk. In fact, much of the diarrhea occurring in cats, especially in kittens, results from the consumption of cow's milk. Cats should also not be fed an all-fish diet.

- Always provide your pet with an adequate supply of clean water.

- Exercise is essential for your dog or cat. The amount needed depends on the breed, age and underlying medical condition. Adequate exercise is always beneficial; it can lessen your pet's destructive behavior, as well as keep your pet in good physical shape and more satisfied with life indoors. And for the safety of everyone—dogs and people alike—please pick up and dispose of your dog's waste.

- *All* dogs and cats should be indoor companions, living as members of the family. It's simply not fair to leave a dog alone in the yard most of the time, and it's worse to chain a dog outside for long periods of time. Such dogs often become aggressive and dangerous. Don't allow your dog or cat to roam outside on their own. Your pet can be hit by a car, be injured by other animals, eat poisonous materials, contract and spread diseases (including rabies), get lost or stolen or become a victim of abuse. Outdoor cats also kill birds and small mammals, and animal bites (particularly dog bites) affect millions of people annually.

- Your dog or cat will benefit from regular grooming. Brush and comb your pet's coat to keep it healthy and free of matted hair.

- Ask your veterinarian to show you how to safely clip your pet's nails and care for ears safely. Provide a scratching post for your cat.

- Regular grooming will also allow you to detect skin problems and parasites such as fleas and ticks. (See page 81 for information on tick removal.) Dogs and cats with fleas often bite and scratch themselves excessively. If you notice excessive scratching or biting, look for evidence of fleas. If your pet has fleas, you may actually see the fleas on your pet or you may see *flea dirt*—tiny black specks that turn reddish when moistened. Before using flea or tick products, talk to your veterinarian about how to treat your pet and your pet's environment safely. Remember that pesticides used to kill fleas are poisons; exercise caution. Make sure you read all labels and follow directions carefully. Be extremely careful not to use a product more frequently or in higher concentrations or volume than directed on the label. Never use these products for an age group or animal not specifically mentioned on the label. If you're using more than one product (that includes using a flea collar and a dip, as well as more than one kind of flea insecticide), or if you're using a professional exterminator, make sure the insecticides you're using are compatible and completely safe to use in combination. Don't use pesticides on extremely young, old, sick, pregnant or heartworm-infected animals.

- Good grooming includes regular teeth cleaning at home. Your veterinarian can show you how to care for your pet's teeth and may recommend cleaning and scaling at the veterinary clinic.

THE HIDDEN DISEASE: PET OVERPOPULATION

You may not think of pet overpopulation as a disease, but it kills millions of dogs and cats each year. This is a disease for which there is a cure: spaying (for females) or neutering (for males). This cure also provides health and behavioral benefits for your pet.

- When performed early, spaying can prevent breast cancer (mammary tumors). Spaying at any age eliminates the risk of uterine infections, uterine or ovarian cancer and some skin disorders. Neutering can prevent testicular disease and greatly lessen the risk of prostate disease. The American Veterinary Medical Association and others agree it is safe to spay or neuter most puppies and kittens as early as eight weeks of age. *It is not better for your female pet's health to delay spaying until after her first heat or to let her have a litter before spaying!*

- Spayed or neutered pets are less likely to roam, spray or mark territory or be aggressive, although neutering will not affect a dog's instinct to protect their human family. Pets who are spayed or neutered are generally better, more affectionate companions, and neither you nor your pet need to suffer through the physical and behavioral problems associated with heat cycles.

- There is a myth that spayed or neutered pets automatically become fat and lazy. On the contrary, you can keep your pet lively and trim through proper diet and exercise.

- In many studies of serious dog bites, evidence shows that bites are more often inflicted by unneutered dogs.

A Lost Pet's Ticket Home: ID

- Even though your pet should live indoors and remain under your supervision when outside, pets should wear collars and up-to-date identification at all times. You never know when someone will leave a door or gate open, or when you and your pet might inadvertently become separated. If your pet becomes lost, a tag with your name, address and phone number can help reunite you and your pet.

- Affix license or rabies tags to your pet's collar as required by state or local law. For pets with medical problems, you can add a tag with essential medical information.

- When you travel with your pet, your dog or cat should wear a temporary tag with a contact name and number or the number where you'll be staying.

- Some people choose to tattoo their pets. While the mark is permanent, it is less effective than an ID tag in helping an animal's finder reach the animal's owner.

- A microchip is a high-tech device that can provide another form of identification. About the size of a grain of rice, the microchip is implanted by a veterinarian or animal shelter under your animal's skin. The microchip contains a code number that identifies your pet for life. The code number is detected by a scanner which displays the information contained in the chip. Because the microchip cannot be seen by the naked eye and because there have been problems with the technology, a microchip should only be used as a back-up form of identification.

- If you do lose your dog or cat, don't depend entirely on any method of identification. Begin to search for your pet immediately, contact your local animal shelter and ask them for tips on how to find your pet and who else you should contact.

TRAVELING WITH YOUR PET

- If you're moving to a new area, you will, of course, be taking your pet with you. You simply need to consider the best and safest mode of travel for your dog or cat.

- If you're thinking about taking your pet on vacation with you, you have to consider your pet's overall health, whether your pet likes to travel, where you'll be staying, the time of year, your options if you don't take your pet with you and whether taking your pet on a vacation is really in their best interest.

- Before any trip, have your pet examined by your veterinarian. Get any required legal travel documents, make sure vaccinations are up to date and get any medications your pet might need. (Medications used specifically for travel should be given to your pet on a trial basis several days before you leave to make sure your pet doesn't suffer adverse effects.)

- If you're traveling by car, take your pet's travel kit (see the next section). Keep a supply of water in the car and be prepared to make frequent rest stops. Never let your pet out of the car without proper restraint. Inside the car, keep your cat in a carrier; dogs should be in carriers or restrained in a harness. Don't let your dog ride with their head out the window. Finally, never leave your pets in a parked car where they will be vulnerable to heat distress or theft.

- Although thousands of pets fly on airlines without problems, there are still risks involved. Don't fly your pets unless it's absolutely necessary. If you must, make your travel arrangements well in advance and ask about all regulations, including any quarantine requirements at your destination. If you have a small pet, try to make arrangements to take the animal on board with you. If your pet must travel in the cargo area, use direct flights; travel on the same flight as your pet; ask to watch your pet being loaded and unloaded; and when you board the plane, notify the captain and at least one flight attendant that your pet is in the cargo hold.

- If you choose to leave your pet behind while you go on vacation, be sure whoever is caring for your pet has your vacation phone number, complete feeding and care instructions and the number of your veterinarian. It is also a good idea to tell your veterinarian who will be caring for your pet and what your wishes are for veterinary care in case of emergency while you're gone.

WHAT TO PACK FOR YOUR PET

There are a number of essentials to take when you travel with your pet or if you must evacuate with your pet in a disaster: medications, medical records, food, bowls, first aid kit, bedding, litter and litter box, leash, collar and tags, grooming supplies, current pet photo (in case your pet gets lost), a favorite toy or two and, especially for cats, a sturdy and well ventilated carrier.

PREPARE FOR DISASTER

- Disasters can strike anytime, anywhere. Whether your family is affected by a natural disaster, hazardous material spill or a fire, every member of your family (including your pets) will have a better chance of survival if you have a disaster plan ahead of time.

- If you have to evacuate your home for any reason, even if you don't expect to be gone for long, *take your pets with you.*

- Red Cross disaster shelters cannot accept pets because of states' health and safety regulations and other considerations (except for service animals who assist people with disabilities), so your disaster plan should include places you and your pets can stay while you're out of your home.

- Have a portable pet disaster supplies kit ready to go. (See the previous section, *What to Pack For Your Pet.*)

- If you have warning of an impending disaster, bring your pets inside. *Never* leave a dog chained in the yard.

- Since disasters may strike when you're away from home, find a trusted neighbor who would be willing to evacuate your pets and meet you at a prearranged location. This person should be comfortable with your pets, know where your animals are likely to be, know where your disaster supplies kit is kept (including the pet's carrier) and have a key to your home.

A FINAL FAREWELL

Inevitably the time will come when you must say good-bye to your beloved companion animal. Your veterinarian can help you decide if and when euthanasia is necessary to ease your pet's suffering. You must also be prepared for the fact that injuries and accidents often result in death, even when first aid measures are taken promptly and correctly and even after treatment by a veterinarian. Losing your pet, for any reason, is no different for most people than losing any member of your family, so allow yourself to grieve and don't be embarrassed about seeking support. Many local humane societies and veterinarians can offer advice about grief counseling.

OWNERS WITH SERIOUS MEDICAL CONDITIONS

People with serious medical conditions are often led to believe they should give up their pets. For example, people with compromised immune systems may be more susceptible to some kinds of infections from some animals. Giving up beloved companion animals isn't the only option, though. If you or someone who spends time with your pets has a compromised immune system from HIV infection or certain kidney or liver diseases, or from treatments or drugs that suppress the immune system, or have had a bone–marrow transplant, there are simple precautions that can reduce the chance of infection from your pets.

Talk to your veterinarian about what you can do to keep yourself, other people, and your pets healthy. Most of all, have hope—you may be able to keep your pet. Sometimes love is the best medicine of all.

For more information on HIV/AIDS Prevention Education, contact your local Red Cross. For those with HIV/AIDS who want more information on care for your pets, contact any of the following organizations:

- PAWS (Pets Are Wonderful Support)—Los Angeles
  (213) 876-7297
- PAWS—San Francisco
  (415) 241-1460
- PETS—D.C.
  (202) 234-PETS
- POWARS (Pet Owners With AIDS Resource Service)—New York
  (212) 246-6307

Index

Superficial 43

C

D

EMERGENCY INFORMATION

IN CASE OF DISASTER

If you must evacuate in a disaster, take your pet with you. Because Red Cross shelters don't accept pets (except service dogs), be sure to locate a safe place for your pets in advance, before disaster strikes, and record the information here:

Pet-friendly hotel/motel: _____

Address/phone: _____

Boarding kennel: _____

Address/phone: _____

Animal hospital for boarding: _____

Address/phone: _____

Friend/petsitter: _____

Address/phone: _____

PET HEALTH RECORD

Pet's Name: _____   Species: _____

Breed or Type: _____   Age as of _____ : _____
                                      (month/year)   (age)

Sex: _____   Date Spayed/Neutered: _____

Color/markings: _____

Other Pets' Names: _____   Species: _____

Breed or Type: _____   Age as of _____ : _____
                                      (month/year)   (age)

Sex: _____   Date Spayed/Neutered: _____

Color/markings: _____

Veterinarian: _____

Address/phone: _____

Emergency hospital: _____

Address/phone: _____

National Animal Poison Control Center: 1-800-548-2423 or 1-900-680-0000
(Note: There are fees associated with their services.)

IMMUNIZATIONS

Enter the immunizations your pet receives below; note the type, year, and date.

Pet: _____   Date/Year

Rabies							

Pet: _____   Date/Year

Rabies							

OTHER MEDICAL INFORMATION

Enter dates and types of major surgery or illness.

_____

_____

_____

_____

_____

AMERICAN RED CROSS HEALTH AND SAFETY TRAINING

The American Red Cross offers a variety of health and safety training opportunities and resources to help you prepare for emergencies. For more information, contact your local Red Cross chapter or visit www.redcross.org.

First Aid and CPR/AED for Communities and Schools

Community First Aid and Safety

First Aid—Responding to Emergencies

Sport Safety Training

First Aid and CPR/AED for Workplaces

* First Aid/CPR/AED Program
* Bloodborne Pathogens Training: Preventing Disease Transmission

Injury-Control Modules

First Aid and CPR/AED Programs for Professional Rescuers

Emergency Response

CPR/AED for the Professional Rescuer

Oxygen Administration

First Aid for Youth

Basic Aid Training

First Aid for Children Today

Babysitter's Training

Emergency and Disaster Preparedness and Education

Together We Prepare—First Aid and Preparedness

* First Aid and Emergency Preparedness Quick Reference
* First Aid Fast booklet

First Aid Kits

Emergency Preparedness Kits

Aquatics Training

Parent and Child Aquatics

Learn-to-Swim

Swimming and Water Safety Education Materials

Longfellow's WHALE Tales

Water Safety Instructor Training

Safety Training for Swim Coaches

GuardStart

Lifeguard Training

Lifeguard Management

Aquatic Examiner Service

Caregiver Training

Family Caregiving

Nurse Assistant Training

* Available in Spanish

MISSION OF THE AMERICAN RED CROSS

The American Red Cross, a humanitarian organization led by volunteers and guided by its Congressional Charter and the Fundamental Principles of the International Red Cross Movement, will provide relief to victims of disaster and help people prevent, prepare for, and respond to emergencies.

FUNDAMENTAL PRINCIPLES OF THE INTERNATIONAL RED CROSS AND RED CRESCENT MOVEMENT

HUMANITY

IMPARTIALITY

NEUTRALITY

INDEPENDENCE

VOLUNTARY SERVICE

UNITY

UNIVERSALITY

When Seconds Count, Help is at Your Fingertips!

First Aid and Emergency Preparedness
Quick Reference Guide
Stock No. 652138
Retail Price: $9.95

I n an emergency situation, you need to think fast—and act even faster. This quick reference guide from the American Red Cross provides you with lifesaving information right at your fingertips.

- Step-by-step directions for responding to a variety of first aid emergencies and sudden illnesses
- Color photographs and easy-to-read instructions
- Information for preparing for disasters from fires to floods to tornadoes

Order your quick reference guide today by visiting www.redcross.org, contacting your local Red Cross chapter or calling (800) 667-2968.

Together, we can save a life

A MediMedia USA Company